ENGLISH BRAINSTORMERS!

Ready-to-Use Games and Activities That Make Language Skills Fun to Learn

Jack Umstatter

illustrated by Maureen Umstatter

JOSSEY-BASS
A Wiley Imprint
www.josseybass.com

Published by Jossey-Bass
A Wiley Imprint
989 Market Street, San Francisco, CA 94103-1741   www.josseybass.com

Jossey-Bass books and products are available through most bookstores. To contact Jossey-Bass directly call our Customer Care Department within the U.S. at 800-956-7739, outside the U.S. at 317-572-3986 or fax 317-572-4002.

Jossey-Bass also publishes its books in a variety of electronic formats. Some content that appears in print may not be available in electronic books.

Library of Congress Cataloging-in-Publication Data has been applied for.

ISBN 0–7879–6583–9

Printed in the United States of America
FIRST EDITION
PB Printing   10 9 8 7 6 5 4 3 2 1

DEDICATION

Dedicated, once again, to Chris, Kate, and Maureen—with love

ACKNOWLEDGMENTS

Special thanks to my daughter Maureen for her artistic talents in illustrating yet another book!

Again, I appreciate the many hours of help extended by my wife, Chris, throughout this writing.

Thanks to my daughter Kate for her continued inspiration.

My sincere thanks to my editor, Bernice Golden, for her knowledge and guidance during this writing process.

For my good friend Tom Hall, I thank you for your expertise and efforts in forming the critical-thinking activities.

My appreciation also extends to former students, Kira Licata and Nora McGeough, for their writings found in activities 163 and 164.

ABOUT THE AUTHOR

Jack Umstatter has taught English on both the junior high school and senior high school levels since 1972. He has also taught Education at Dowling College in Oakdale, New York, for the past twelve years. Mr. Umstatter currently teaches English in the Cold Spring Harbor School District on Long Island.

Mr. Umstatter graduated from Manhattan College with a B.A. in English and completed his M.A. in English at S.U.N.Y–Stony Brook. He earned his Educational Administration degree at Long Island University.

Selected Teacher of the Year several times, Mr. Umstatter was also elected to *Who's Who Among America's Teachers*. Most recently, he has appeared in *Contemporary Authors*. Mr. Umstatter has taught all levels of secondary English classes including the Honors and Advanced Placement classes. As coach of the high school's academic team, the Brainstormers, he led the team in capturing the Long Island and New York State championships when competing in the American Scholastic Competition Network National Tournament of Champions in Lake Forest, Illinois. His teams have recently competed in the Questions Unlimited National Academic Championships in New Orleans and Los Angeles.

Mr. Umstatter's other publications include *Hooked on Literature!* (1994), 201 *Ready-to-Use Word Games for the English Classroom* (1994), *Brain Games!* (1996), *Hooked on English!* (1997), the six-volume *Writing Skills Curriculum Library* (1999), and *Grammar Grabbers!* (2000), all published by Jossey-Bass. He also wrote *Where Words Come From* (2002), published by Franklin Watts, a division of Scholastic/Grolier Publishers.

ABOUT THIS RESOURCE

Lately, we teachers have been bombarded with educational terminology such as "The State Standards," "Learning Assessments," "Academic Intervention Services," and "Competency Evaluation." Yes, the new standards are probably necessary for some students for a number of reasons. Yes, students who are not performing up to a specific standard should be given remediation. Few would argue against either. Yet, through all of these assessments and evaluations, many teachers confess that the joy of teaching, the "fun in the classroom," has been slowly disappearing. Instead, pressure and stress for both you and your students have appeared. How often have you heard, or even said it yourself, "There is little time for anything other than preparing my students for all these assessments!"? In a nutshell, we need to make learning fun again—both for ourselves as teachers and, more importantly, for our kids as learners.

Plain and simple: Students love fun activities. Because of the many and varied skills that we are asked to teach our students each day, the classroom is an ideal place to incorporate fun activities to introduce and review the various language arts skills including grammar, mechanics, word development, vocabulary, research, critical thinking, and creative writing, to name just a few.

Fun involvement—what a wonderful way to achieve classroom goals and improve language arts skills at the same time! Will our students' test scores suffer because we include some games and other enjoyable and worthwhile activities in our curriculum? No! Studies support the fact that students retain more when they are actively involved or have "hands on" in the learning process. Through such activities, students will certainly absorb more information as they learn, review, and retain concepts in your classroom. Plus, they will be enjoying themselves at the same time! What a great combination!

The 181 entertaining activities in *English Brainstormers!* will make your students' time in the classroom informative, enjoyable, and entertaining. Students will look forward to these creative, ready-to-use, classroom-tested activities. These learning activities can function as introductions, reinforcements, or homework assignments. They can be used as individual, group, or whole-class activities. Many of these activities will serve as time-fillers or extra-credit assignments. Formatted as crosswords, word finds, riddles, magic squares, word generators, jumbles, and more, these learning activities will motivate your students to think more astutely and want to do their best in the process.

The resource is divided into seven sections, as follows:

- Section One, "This Is Not Your Grandma's Grammar," includes 29 activities designed to review and reinforce parts of speech, verbals, phrases, clauses, sentences, spelling, diction, syntax, mechanics, and plurals.

- Vocabulary, prefixes, roots, suffixes, word construction, synonyms, antonyms, word and phrase etymologies, and word recognition comprise the 29 activities in Section Two, "Playing with Words." Students will become more word curious, "word wise," and more confident in their everyday writing and speech.

- The 26 activities in the third section, "Getting Set for the Standards," will help your students become more versatile and intelligent learners and test-takers. These activities include work with synonyms, quotes, topic sentences, essays, word expressions, spelling, vocabulary, the cloze method of reading, and mechanics. Students will also perform tasks similar to those found on typical standardized tests.

- In the fourth section, "Really Writing and Really Discussing," students will work on the 24 activities that include poetry interpretation, literary and character analysis, creative thinking, idioms, expository writing, creative story writing, and discussion. Here they will compare their views on many interesting topics and issues. An examination of the techniques and styles of various writers is also found in this section.

- Section Five, "Critical Thinking Is Critical!" presents 25 activities designed to improve students' critical-thinking skills. Exercises involving word origins, word play, spoonerisms, imagination, logic application, character analysis, examining evidence, associative thinking, creative thinking, and other interesting real-world applications are found within this section.

- The sixth section, "Researching and Remembering," incorporates many of the concepts and tasks necessary to write reports and deliver speeches on various topics. Grouping pieces of biographical, literary, historical, or geographical information, researching elements of the English language, comparing and contrasting different literary genres, working with quotations, finding information about famous people, and assessing a literary situation are just some of the 23 games and activities that your students will enjoy here.

- "You Are Special!" is the concluding section. Many of these 25 activities focus on the students and the world around them. Whether it is a personal inventory exercise, a descriptive personal writing, an autobiographical sketch, a "most important moments" list, an evaluation of various literary characters, a personal decision-making activity, or a look at what the students think about themselves and others, these activities are designed to make your students think more maturely and insightfully as they assess the world around them.

It was William Butler Yeats who said, "Education is not filling a pail, but lighting a fire." You will light that fire, and your students will be filled with enthusiasm as they do these activities. I know. My students do. Yours will, too. Enjoy!

Jack Umstatter

CONTENTS

SECTION TWO

PLAYING WITH WORDS   37

SECTION THREE

GETTING SET FOR THE STANDARDS   73

SECTION FOUR
REALLY WRITING AND REALLY DISCUSSING   109

SECTION FIVE
CRITICAL THINKING IS CRITICAL! 139

SECTION SIX

RESEARCHING AND REMEMBERING   171

SECTION SEVEN
YOU ARE SPECIAL 203

TEACHER NOTE

You will need the following information in order for students to complete Activity 87 "Examining Emily," Activity 96 "Funeral Blues," and Activity 98 "Towns":

Activity 87: Emily Dickinson's poem "Number 315" can be found in *The Complete Works of Emily Dickinson* edited by Thomas Johnson (Boston: Little, Brown, and Company, 1976). It is also available on the Internet at:

www.belmont.edu/Humanities/literature/English221/315/web.html   OR

www.csustan.edu/english/reuben/pal/chap4/dickinson_301-400.html

Activity 96: W. H. Auden's poem "Funeral Blues" is available at:

http://www.egr.unlv.edu/~rho/interests/other/poems/w.h.auden/funeral.blues.html

Activity 98: Lyrics for Bruce Springsteen's "My Hometown" can be found at:

www.reallyrics.com/lyrics/B008400010099.asp

The web address for Billy Joel's "Allentown" is:

www.reallyrics.com/lyrics/B004900010004.asp

Josey-Bass has provided these websites for teacher use only. The publisher cannot guarantee the accuracy or completeness of the information found in these sites and is not responsible for errors or omissions or results obtained from use of the information.

Section One

THIS IS NOT YOUR GRANDMA'S GRAMMAR

1. SCAN, SORT, AND EARN

At least 35 present or past tense verbs can be found in this puzzle. *Scan*, *sort*, and *earn* are three such words. The letters of each word must be in a box either adjacent to or diagonal to each other. Though the same letter can be used twice in a word, no letter can be used consecutively. You must move from one letter to another. Write your words on another sheet of paper. Each word is worth 1 point. So *scan* the puzzle, *sort* the letters, and *earn* your points!

K	O	S	C	A
R	O	H	R	N
T	D	E	A	T
E	I	B	L	K

2. LINKING IT UP

The 25 verbs and verb phrases listed below can be found forward, backward, or diagonally in this word-find puzzle. Some phrases contain a single word, while others contain two or even three words. Find the verbs and phrases in the puzzle and circle them. Then, on another sheet of paper, use any 15 of your circled answers in 15 sentences you compose.

c	a	n	b	e	d	l	k	w	e	r	e	a	p	p	e	a	r	h
s	r	g	m	n	e	l	n	q	b	m	b	w	w	l	t	m	e	a
v	h	r	u	e	z	e	f	c	s	j	l	i	o	o	s	p	m	d
h	d	o	f	r	r	m	i	s	t	s	l	l	u	o	a	m	a	b
p	s	w	u	a	l	s	n	z	a	e	a	l	l	k	t	l	i	e
y	h	n	m	l	v	w	j	w	y	e	h	b	d	b	c	b	n	e
h	a	q	b	l	d	k	h	t	m	m	s	e	h	q	v	r	x	n
m	v	k	t	s	k	b	l	d	a	w	h	h	a	s	b	e	e	n
x	e	b	b	m	j	w	e	y	y	p	l	q	v	j	m	f	z	x
s	b	d	v	r	x	q	p	v	b	c	r	v	e	d	h	x	y	c
h	e	b	e	c	o	m	e	l	e	j	v	s	b	h	x	r	p	w
d	e	c	b	p	t	p	c	h	w	g	g	f	e	t	h	y	h	r
b	n	k	q	z	g	x	t	q	v	m	k	p	e	k	v	q	d	g
v	c	m	d	z	z	x	y	m	j	h	y	j	n	c	j	d	v	h

am	have been	sound
appear	is	stay
are	look	taste
become	maybe	was
can be	remain	were
feel	seem	will be
grow	shall be	would have been
had been	should be	
has been	smell	

3. LISTEN TO YOURSELF

Your ears (and those of your teacher and classmates) are very important in this activity. Why? You are asked to name nouns, verbs (present tense only), and adjectives. Sounds easy so far, doesn't it? The key here is that you must name them according to the number of syllables in the word. Thus, if you are asked for a one-syllable noun, *cat* is fine. A three-syllable verb? *Minimize*. A four-syllable adjective? *Intelligent*. Use your dictionary or thesaurus if necessary. So listen to yourself, and have a good time!

Name:

4 one-syllable nouns _____

4 one-syllable verbs _____

4 one-syllable adjectives _____

Name:

4 two-syllable nouns _____

4 two-syllable verbs _____

4 two-syllable adjectives _____

Name:

4 three-syllable nouns _____

4 three-syllable verbs _____

4 three-syllable adjectives _____

Name:

4 four-syllable nouns _____

4 four-syllable verbs _____

4 four-syllable adjectives _____

4. ADJECTIVE HUNT

You have 2 minutes to circle the 25 adjectives in these columns. Score 4 points for each correct answer. Who will score the highest? Perhaps you will. Good luck!

along	hiss	really
answers	impressive	recently
apostrophe	independent	reliable
apprehensive	interesting	restore
because	large	scent
bigger	last	sentence
biographical	lost	similar
comma	manliness	soft
conclusive	masterful	soluble
controversial	meaning	someone
definitive	neighbor	statement
effort	occasion	strong
everyone	orderly	supplementary
fraction	past	sweltering
furthermore	poetry	voluntarily
gobble	pronounced	voluntary
guiding	punctuate	

Score: _____ points

5. MOVE IT ON!

The object of the game is simple: You just have to MOVE IT ON! In the appropriate column, write words that fit the description; however, you must start the next word in the column with the last letter of the previous word. For example, for "4-letter verbs," an appropriate sequence of words would be *grow, want, take, etch, haul, lend, drip, prod, deal, loan,* and so forth. No word can be repeated in any column. Your teacher will decide whether "Move It On!" will be played as a class or individually. Either way, have fun!

5-letter verbs	3-letter adjectives	3-letter verbs	5-letter adjectives
_____	_____	_____	_____
_____	_____	_____	_____
_____	_____	_____	_____
_____	_____	_____	_____
_____	_____	_____	_____
_____	_____	_____	_____
_____	_____	_____	_____
_____	_____	_____	_____
_____	_____	_____	_____
_____	_____	_____	_____

6. VERBS AND PRONOUNS GALORE!

Draw a circle around 10 verbs and a box around 10 pronouns in the list below. Each correct answer is worth 5 points. Write your score in the space below.

affections	false	kick	ode	solidarity
anxiety	firmness	main	ourselves	species
are	fix	maltreat	psalm	stand
author	fortitude	manhood	punishment	stereotype
before	gallantry	melt	quite	them
begin	had	mine	quotations	tremor
consonance	he	myself	reality	varying
couplet	I	nobody	seize	way
definitions	interpretation	none	several	whole
each	irately	octagon	since	zoology

Score: _____ points

7. AND THE OTHERS?

The word *down* can be used as five different parts of speech, which might be the record! Here is your chance to show what other words might (or might not) give *down* some competition. At least one part of speech is given for each word below. Your job is to give the word's other parts of speech. Write your answers after the word. Although three lines are provided for each word, you might not have to use all of them. *Hint*: For one of these words, you will have to use an additional line because it, like *down*, can be used as five parts of speech.

1. **mess** (*verb*): noun _____ _____

2. **even** (*adjective*): _____ _____ _____

3. **close** (*noun*): _____ _____ _____

4. **right** (*verb*): _____ _____ _____

5. **spirit** (*noun*): _____ _____ _____

6. **turn** (*verb*): _____ _____ _____

7. **register** (*verb*): _____ _____ _____

8. **set** (*verb*) _____ _____ _____

9. **grass** (*noun*): _____ _____ _____

10. **lead** (*verb*): _____ _____ _____

11. **friend** (*noun*): _____ _____ _____

12. **head** (*verb*): _____ _____ _____

13. **contact** (*noun*): _____ _____ _____

14. **hit** (*adjective*): _____ _____ _____

15. **plane** (*adjective*): _____ _____ _____

8. PROBING FOR PRONOUNS

Each of the 24 answers to this crossword puzzle contains a pronoun. For example, the answer to 2 Across, *gone*, contains the pronoun *one*. Write the answers to these clues and circle the pronoun in each answer. The first letter of each answer has been filled in for you. Enjoy probing for these other 23 pronouns.

8. PROBING FOR PRONOUNS (continued)

Across
2. wedge-shaped piece of wood used for filling a space
4. overwhelming
7. type of park or song
11. to perceive through the ears
13. nonsensical
17. a nobody
18. cereal grass

Down
1. vehicle
2. storage unit
3. opposite of out
5. dry's opposite
6. fruit
8. sixty minutes
9. damp
10. time deadline
12. nearly
14. friend
15. in an unkind way
16. capable

9. PLENTY OF PREPOSITIONS

Here are 20 prepositions for you to unscramble. Several letters have been filled in. You are to fill in the other letters for each preposition. Use the Letter Substitution Code below. (Note that the letters J, K, Q, X, Y, and Z are not used in the code.)

1. RARDCEH = A G A __ __ __ __
2. TPVS = __ V __ __
3. MVBTN = __ __ __ __ __
4. FTNC = __ __ __ __
5. MVUTSV = __ __ __ __ __ __
6. DCHT = __ __ __ __
7. WREH = __ A __ __
8. RMTPV = A__ __ V__
9. TU = __ __
10. RMTIH = A__ __ __ __
11. ICFVS = __ __ __ __ __
12. MVODCF = __ __ __ __ __ __
13. RH = A __
14. FISDCA = __ __ __ __ __ G
15. USTL = __ __ __ __
16. NDHO = __ __ __ __
17. RUHVS = A__ __ __ __
18. UTS = __ __ __
19. HOSTIAOTIH = __ __ __ __ __ G __ __ __ __
20. RGSTEE = A __ __ __ __ __

Letter Substitution Code

Code:	A	B	C	D	E	F	G	H	I	L	M	N	O	P	R	S	T	U	V	W
Real:	G														A				E	

12

10. IT'S ALL IN THE FAMILY

Each of the 30 words hidden in this word-find puzzle is all from the same family of words. They are all prepositions! These 30 words can be found backward, forward, diagonally, and vertically. Circle the 30 prepositions.

```
a  b  o  v  e  u  p  o  n  h  z  c  x  a  b  o  a  r  d  w
k  r  k  t  l  p  j  k  s  h  o  f  f  a  m  o  n  g  h  v
x  m  j  t  b  w  q  m  n  n  d  c  t  a  z  f  m  s  c  h
h  n  x  x  m  c  s  s  c  j  w  j  b  h  n  d  r  s  c  y
t  d  m  w  h  h  v  e  z  b  v  o  h  x  o  j  b  o  t  r
a  o  h  b  i  i  r  y  v  u  u  x  t  k  n  e  r  r  m  w
e  l  w  s  i  n  c  e  y  t  a  m  i  d  t  p  e  c  x  e
n  l  f  a  i  s  s  b  r  y  z  p  w  w  o  d  g  a  s  j
e  r  q  n  r  l  n  i  m  z  b  t  e  f  i  m  a  t  d  q
b  a  g  p  f  d  d  b  d  q  v  e  b  s  g  z  r  h  b  f
l  e  h  t  s  n  y  w  c  e  n  b  e  l  o  w  d  r  x  q
m  n  f  f  u  w  j  j  k  n  n  b  y  q  j  w  i  o  w  d
p  p  n  o  j  o  p  i  h  h  d  h  o  w  s  x  n  u  y  t
v  c  r  t  r  d  l  d  s  z  f  v  n  q  y  q  g  g  z  t
b  a  p  f  r  e  g  t  l  w  g  n  d  h  m  y  k  h  y  z
```

aboard	around	beyond	from	regarding
about	before	but	in	since
above	below	by	inside	through
across	beneath	concerning	like	toward
amid	beside	down	near	upon
among	between	except	onto	with

11. SEEING ALLITERATIVELY

Let's take an imaginary trip. The rules are simple. Next to each letter, write a two-word phrase that has both words starting with that letter and each word having at least 5 letters. You must be able to "see" what the phrase describes. For example, you could write *agile antelope* for the letter A. Be sure to use an adjective followed by a noun.

A _____   N _____

B _____   O _____

C _____   P _____

D _____   Q _____

E _____   R _____

F _____   S _____

G _____   T _____

H _____   U _____

I _____   V _____

J _____   W _____

K _____   X _____

L _____   Y _____

M _____   Z _____

12. HOW VERSATILE ARE THESE WORDS?

Each of the ten words below can function as at least one part of speech. How many can function as two, three, or more? Circle the two-letter combination next to each part of speech that the word can be. Then write the two-letter combinations in order on the line at the bottom of the page. If your answers are correct, you will have answered the riddle. Good luck!

1. **down:** (ON) preposition, (TO) pronoun, (EW) adverb, (IS) conjunction, (AT) adjective, (CH) verb, (ES) noun

2. **happy:** (RE) noun, (ST) verb, (OO) preposition, (CE) adjective

3. **rejoiced:** (TR) adjective, (EE) adverb, (LL) verb

4. **snowy:** (PO,) verb, (S,) adjective, (T,) noun

5. **run:** (AN) adjective, (DT) noun, (ER) adverb, (ST) conjunction, (HE) verb

6. **immature:** (OT) adjective, (LT) adverb, (NN) noun

7. **light:** (EE) conjunction, (HE) adjective, (RS) verb, (EL) noun, (SS) preposition

8. **part:** (UR) interjection, (IE) adverb, (LS) verb, (WA) noun

9. **outline:** (TC) noun, (HE) verb, (SE) adjective, (OO) adverb

10. **fantastic:** (S!) adjective, (T!) adverb, (R!) noun

The riddle: What is the difference between a prison guard and a jeweler?

_____

_____

13. GRAMMAR TERMS ON PARADE

Match the underlined words with their grammatical names found below the paragraph. Use each term and each underlined portion only once per reading selection.

Selection One:
"Now her departure <u>for Bettsbridge</u> <u>had once more eased</u> his mind, and all his thoughts were on the prospect of his evening with Mattie. <u>Only</u> one thing weighed <u>on him</u>, and that was having told Zeena that he was to receive the cash for the lumber. He foresaw <u>so clearly</u> the consequences of this imprudence that with considerable reluctance he decided to ask Andrew Hale for a small advance on his loan." From *Ethan Frome* by Edith Wharton

Adjective phrase _____

Verb phrase _____

Adverb _____

Adverb phrase _____

Consecutive adverbs _____

Selection Two:
"Back <u>in the days</u> <u>when everyone was old or stupid or young and foolish</u> and me and Sugar were the only ones <u>just</u> right, <u>this</u> lady moved on our block with <u>nappy</u> hair and proper speech <u>and</u> no makeup." From "The Lesson" by Toni Cade Bambara

Adverb phrase _____

Adverb _____

Conjunction _____

Pronoun/adjective _____

Adjective _____

Clause _____

14. PARTS-OF-SPEECH MAGIC SQUARE

Match each word in Group A with its description in Group B. Each word is used only once. Write the correct number in the correct square. If your answers are correct, all columns, rows, and the two diagonals add up to the same number. One has been given to help you get started.

A =	B = 16	C =	D =	E =
F =	G =	H =	I =	J =
K =	L =	M =	N =	O =
P =	Q =	R =	S =	T =
U =	V =	W =	X =	Y =

14. PARTS-OF-SPEECH MAGIC SQUARE (continued)

Group A

A. who	F. informative	K. swell	P. deer	U. very
B. schoolhouse	G. radar	L. down	Q. should	V. set
C. Detroit	H. wider	M. into	R. it	W. we
D. read	I. mine	N. and	S. tallest	X. myself
E. jury	J. hah	O. can't	T. name	Y. went

Group B

1. neuter pronoun
2. present and past tense verb
3. contraction
4. adverb
5. palindromic noun
6. verb, adjective, and noun
7. noun and present, past, and past participle verb form
8. comparative adjective form
9. superlative adjective form
10. collective noun
11. noun, verb, and possessive pronoun
12. verb and noun
13. interrogative pronoun
14. noun, verb, adjective, adverb, and preposition
15. plural pronoun
16. compound noun
17. preposition
18. reflexive pronoun
19. interjection
20. singular and plural noun
21. past tense of the verb "go"
22. adjective
23. helping verb
24. proper noun
25. conjunction

15. HIDDEN COUNTRIES

Fill in the missing letters of the 20 countries listed below. On the line next to the country, write the part of speech of the word formed from the given bold letters.

1. __ **R A N** __ __ _____

2. **G E R M** __ __ __ _____

3. __ __ **L A N D** _____

4. __ __ **G E N T** __ __ __ _____

5. **C A M E** __ __ __ __ _____

6. __ **P A I N** _____

7. **I T** __ __ __ _____

8. __ __ __ **K E Y** _____

9. **F I N** __ __ __ __ _____

10. **H U N G** __ __ __ _____

11. __ __ __ __ __ **T A N** _____

12. __ __ __ **G A P** __ __ __ _____

13. __ **C O T** __ __ __ __ _____

14. **A N D** __ __ __ __ _____

15. __ **H A D** _____

16. **D E N** __ __ __ __ _____

17. **I R E** __ __ __ __ _____

18. __ **O R** __ __ __ _____

19. __ __ **C A R** __ __ __ __ _____

20. __ __ **R A G** __ __ __ _____

16. VERBALLY SPEAKING

Tell whether each sentence contains a gerund (G), participle (P), or infinitive (I) phrase. Each type of verbal appears five times. To check your answers, know that the numbers of each type of verbal add up to 40.

1. _____ That group wanted to share the duties.

2. _____ To dream about the unknown was one of his most enjoyable activities.

3. _____ Telling the truth has always been very important to him.

4. _____ The pitcher, distracted by the opposition's verbal taunts, was erratic.

5. _____ We heard the bell ringing in the corridor.

6. _____ I cannot stand the banging on the tiles.

7. _____ Painted by the renowned artist, the new mural created quite a controversy.

8. _____ Efficient planning should be one of the committee's goals.

9. _____ The mountain goat, carefully working his way down the hill, was spotted by the farmer.

10. _____ None of the movie directors volunteered to speak at the festival.

11. _____ Acknowledging Henry's group was the principal's goal.

12. _____ Skiing in the Alps is a great experience.

13. _____ Regina loved to visit her relatives in Belgium.

14. _____ You need to familiarize yourself with the new systems.

15. _____ Reeling from the hit, the football player felt quite dizzy for a few minutes.

17. 25 WITH 4 HAVE 2

Strange title? Not when you consider that these 25 words with 4 letters have 2 definitions!
Match each word from Group A with its correct definition from Group B. Write the number
in the magic square's appropriate box. If your answers are correct, all rows, columns, and the
two diagonals will add up to the same number. One has been given to help you get started.
Have fun!

A =	B = 10	C =	D =	E =
F =	G =	H =	I =	J =
K =	L =	M =	N =	O =
P =	Q =	R =	S =	T =
U =	V =	W =	X =	Y =

17. 25 WITH 4 HAVE 2 (continued)

Group A

A. dash	F. host	K. hand	P. post	U. wind
B. cube	G. duck	L. well	Q. will	V. rest
C. slip	H. fine	M. form	R. down	W. head
D. crab	I. cape	N. wake	S. coin	X. bond
E. nose	J. chop	O. lean	T. fall	Y. junk

Group B

1. run quickly; punctuation mark
2. boss; most important
3. season; collapse
4. hole in the ground used to tap an underground supply of water; in good health
5. piece of land projecting out into the water; sleeveless outer garment
6. join together; duty or obligation
7. position; piece of wood or metal used to support a fence
8. shape or outline; organize into
9. slice of lamb; cut with an ax
10. six-sided solid; to raise to the third power
11. penalty; in good health
12. body part; beat by a small margin
13. remainder; relax
14. invent or devise; round piece of metal used as currency
15. body part; group of bananas
16. determination; desire or purpose
17. come out of a sleep; trail left by a boat
18. multitude; innkeeper
19. go quietly or secretly; woman's undergarment
20. flat-bottomed Chinese or Japanese ship; garbage
21. incline; slender
22. small waterfowl; avoid
23. complain; sea creature
24. air in motion; turn
25. soft, fluffy feathers; gulp or eat greedily

18. FIRST NAMES ONLY

There are very few people who are recognizable by their first name only. Thus, if you said Bob or Michelle, there could be many people who have that as a first name. Yet, if your answers are correct in this activity, you will spell out the first names of 2 men and 2 women who are known primarily by only their first names. Write each answer's correct letter in the appropriate space. The consecutive letters will spell out these four famous first names.

1. _____ The operator had **(P)** begun **(Q)** began to place the call.

2. _____ One of the bells **(E)** rang **(F)** rung last night at midnight.

3. _____ Each of her children had **(K)** swam **(L)** swum in that meet.

4. _____ I had **(D)** saw **(E)** seen how they make glass containers at the museum.

5. _____ Had you **(M)** known **(N)** knew that bit of information?

6. _____ When did the shirt **(A)** shrink **(B)** shrunk so badly?

7. _____ Some musicians had **(C)** took **(D)** taken their instruments back to the bus.

8. _____ **(O)** Mike and he **(N)** Mike and him were chosen to represent this county.

9. _____ Neither of the players **(M)** were **(N)** was on the ballot.

10. _____ **(N)** We **(O)** Us drivers need to have better working conditions.

11. _____ Yogi was **(Z)** more short **(A)** shorter than his older brother.

12. _____ The program started off **(E)** well **(F)** good.

13. _____ My dad felt **(K)** uncertainly **(L)** uncertain about the decision they made.

14. _____ The ministers speak **(U)** clear **(V)** clearly during their sermons.

15. _____ Most of the wires were **(H)** lain **(I)** laid by those workers yesterday.

16. _____ All of the pictures had **(S)** fallen **(T)** fell because of yesterday's humidity.

17. _____ When did the ship **(B)** sank **(C)** sink?

18. _____ Every one of the rules **(G)** were **(H)** was followed well by the students.

19. _____ *The Three Musketeers* **(D)** were **(E)** was written many years ago.

20. _____ The comedy team of Burns and Allen **(Q)** were **(R)** was popular in the 1950s.

19. SPELLING THE PLURALS

Write the correct plural of each of these 24 words below in the correct space within the crossword puzzle. Good luck!

Across

2. die
6. crisis
8. bacterium
9. loaf
10. donkey
12. life
14. stimulus
16. ox
19. shelf
20. passerby
21. mouthful

Down

1. goose
2. deer
3. child
4. radius
5. mouse
7. roof
11. spoonful
12. louse
13. echo
15. tooth
17. piano
18. fly

20. MISSPELLINGS

The words listed are misspelled. Spell each misspelled word correctly by writing the answers in the appropriate spaces.

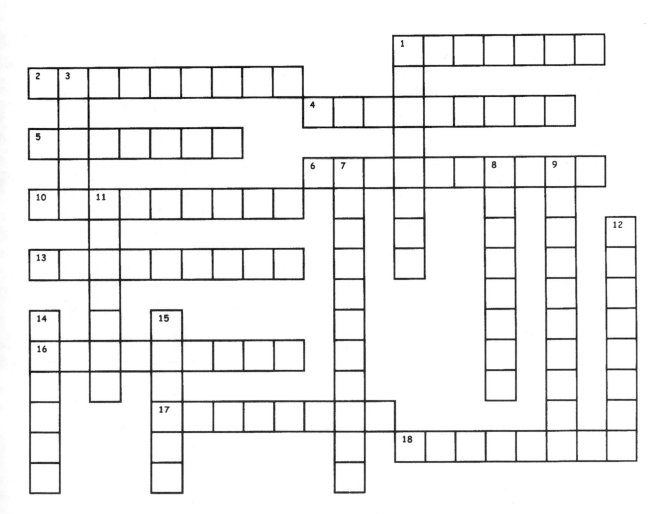

Across

1. forein
2. priviledge
4. curteous
5. higene
6. attendence
10. Wendesday
13. voluntier
16. comunity
17. innferred
18. instence

Down

1. formirely
3. rhime
7. temporment
8. anounse
9. commision
11. dilima
12. sepirite
14. acktuel
15. kwaint

21. FIX UP THESE 20 MISSPELLINGS

The problem here is that there are 20 words (all misspelled) in this word-find puzzle. Circle the "nearly correctly" spelled words and then write the correct spellings on the lines below. Enjoy!

```
f  l  s  x  r  y  q  t  k  f  z  s  t  e  n  n  x  l  t  t
r  d  n  c  b  b  m  d  h  w  s  p  p  n  w  s  n  e  r  b
n  e  e  z  g  x  a  v  g  b  k  q  v  i  x  h  r  g  a  n
t  o  m  v  s  b  l  w  n  s  g  v  k  c  h  m  s  a  n  l
w  p  i  e  i  t  i  k  k  u  l  p  s  e  g  g  r  r  s  r
g  o  h  s  b  d  n  z  k  i  i  y  w  d  r  v  s  u  e  d
p  a  n  q  e  e  t  a  r  t  n  n  e  c  n  o  c  n  c
k  r  x  d  d  y  r  y  a  a  g  d  a  m  e  r  o  s  t  q
x  t  w  w  a  t  n  m  l  v  x  t  y  v  e  l  g  i  l  m
w  i  n  q  l  f  i  w  b  z  f  l  e  s  u  z  n  d  m  l
z  s  r  b  x  d  u  t  z  u  a  i  d  m  y  d  s  e  g  s
y  t  d  w  c  s  j  l  l  m  c  j  f  f  d  q  l  l  l  q
q  i  b  j  w  v  m  v  r  r  q  t  v  c  m  o  j  b  v  w
q  c  j  t  j  r  p  o  e  m  b  a  r  a  s  s  s  m  n  c
l  k  s  p  v  b  f  p  p  r  a  b  a  b  l  y  r  x  l  y
```

_____   _____

_____   _____

_____   _____

_____   _____

_____   _____

_____   _____

_____   _____

_____   _____

22. GRAMMAR AND MECHANICS

Only one sentence in each group is punctuated correctly. Circle the letter of each correct sentence. Be ready to explain why you selected each sentence.

1. **(A)** Brenda, loves to cook, and is very good at it.   **(B)** Brenda loves to cook and she is very good at it.   **(C)** Brenda, who likes to cook, serves delicious dishes.

2. **(A)** Andre Agassi, the tennis player and new father is a friendly man.   **(B)** Manhattan College, the home of the Jaspers, is former mayor Rudy Giuliani's alma mater.
   (C) Arthur Miller, the author of *The Crucible* was once married to Marilyn Monroe.

3. **(A)** During the second inning of the game the crowd erupted in applause.   **(B)** The crowd erupted in applause, during the second inning of the game.   **(C)** During the second inning of the game, the crowd erupted in applause.

4. **(A)** They will however open the doors an hour before the concert.   **(B)** They will however, open the doors an hour before the concert.   **(C)** They will, however, open the doors an hour before the concert.

5. **(A)** She loves to sing "Hey Jude".   **(B)** She loves to sing "Hey Jude."   **(C)** She loves to sing *Hey Jude*.

6. **(A)** "Do you think that Millicent will go to the Junior-Senior Prom with Sylvester?" Anthony asked Paul.   **(B)** "Do you think that Millicent will go to the Junior-Senior Prom with Sylvester," Anthony asked Paul?   **(C)** "Do you think, that Millicent will go to the Junior-Senior Prom with Sylvester?" Anthony asked Paul.

7. **(A)** As long as you know how to write the essay I will not have to help you.   **(B)** As long as you know how to write the essay, I will not have to help you.   **(C)** I will not have to help you, as long as, you know how to write the essay.

8. **(A)** Each of these novels has their good and bad points.   **(B)** Each of these novels has its good and bad points.   **(C)** Both of these novels have their good, and bad, points.

9. **(A)** Henrietta Hornacker is as I see it the one to choose as team captain.
   (B) Henrietta Hornacker is, as I see it, the one to choose as team captain.
   (C) Henrietta Hornacker, is as I see it, the one to choose as team captain.

10. **(A)** "Have you read "A Tale of Two Cities" by Charles Dickens? Millie asked Billy.
    (B) "Have you read "*A Tale of Two Cities*" by Charles Dickens? Millie asked Billy.
    (C) "Have you read *A Tale of Two Cities* by Charles Dickens?" Millie asked Billy.

23. THREE ON A MATCH

How well can you put sentences back together? Each sentence below has been broken up into three parts. Your job is to take one part from each of the three columns and reconstruct the sentence.

Check your answers by writing the consecutive letters of each column on the lines below. The first 10 letters (Column One) spell out PALM and WILLOW. The remaining 20 letters should spell the names of four other trees. Write those names on the appropriate lines.

Column One
1. The EMT (P)
2. The umpire (A)
3. The seagull (L)
4. The surfer (M)
5. The professor (W)
6. The vendor (I)
7. The surgeon (L)
8. The magician (L)
9. The florist (O)
10. The lawyer (W)

Column Two
arranged the flowers (A)
demonstrated the problem (H)
ejected the player (I)
gave the change (C)
lifted the patient (B)
performed the surgery (E)
picked the food (R)
pulled the rabbit (D)
questioned the witness (R)
rode the waves (C)

Column Three
during the trial. (R)
for the wedding. (I)
from the game. (Y)
from the garbage. (P)
in the OR. (S)
into the van. (C)
on the chalkboard. (E)
out of the hat. (F)
to the customer. (S)
toward the shore. (R)

Column One's letters: ___PALM, WILLOW_____

Column Two's letters: _____

Column Three's letters: _____

The 4 trees: _____

28

24. STRUCTURING SENTENCES

You are to write 15 sentences that should be structured according to the instructions below. Label each part. Write your sentences on a separate sheet of paper.

The sentence must include . . .

1. the conjunctions *both* and *and*.

2. the words *hire* and *higher*.

3. a collective noun, a day of the week, and an adverb.

4. all words that begin with the same letter.

5. two pronouns, two subjects, and a day of the week.

6. a pronoun, a conjunction, a color, and a season of the year.

7. a question mark, a plural subject, and a prepositional phrase.

8. a compound verb, a plural subject, a conjunction, a direct object, and a prepositional phrase.

9. an adverb, an adjective, a compound subject, and a prepositional phrase.

10. a prepositional phrase that starts the sentence.

11. an adjective phrase and an infinitive phrase.

12. a question mark, an adverb, an infinitive phrase, and a participle phrase.

13. a contraction, an adverb, and a prepositional phrase.

14. a gerund phrase, a prepositional phrase, an adverb, and an adjective.

15. an adverb, a prepositional phrase, and an indefinite pronoun.

25. WHERE DID THE VOWELS GO?

Each of these sentences has one thing in common: All of their vowels have disappeared! The number under each word indicates how many letters, including the missing vowels, are in that word. Write each sentence on the lines provided. Each word's letters appear in their sequential order.

1. W   cn   g   t   th   str   nw.
    2   3   2   2   3   5   3

_____

_____

2. Sm   ppl   lv   t   sng   nd   dnc.
    4   6   4   2   4   3   5

_____

_____

3. Pls   trn   ff   th   rd.
    6   4   3   3   5

_____

_____

4. Dd   y   fnsh   yr   hmwrk   ssgnmnts?
    3   3   6   4   8   11

_____

_____

5. Thy   hv   nvr   prchsd   ldr   crs.
    4   4   5   9   5   4

_____

_____

25. WHERE DID THE VOWELS GO? (continued)

6. Fls   nd   bs   r   nnyng   t   pcnckrs.
   5   3   4   3   8   2   10

_____

_____

7. Th   wthr   hs   nt   bn   tht   wrm   ths   wk.
   3   7   3   3   4   4   4   4   4

_____

_____

8. Mk   th   ntllgnt   dcsn   sn.
   4   3   11   8   4

_____

_____

On the space below, make up four of your own of these kinds of sentences. Then try them out on your classmates.

_____

_____

_____

_____

_____

_____

_____

_____

_____

26. SENTENCES—LETTER BY LETTER

Each sentence will have as many words as there are letters in the word after the number. The first word starts with the word's first letter, the next word begins with the second letter, the third word with the third letter, and so on. Thus, if the word is *Comb*, a possible sentence could be "Can our match begin?" Only one proper noun is allowed per sentence, and the sentence or question should make sense. After you have finished these ten, you might make up some of your own for your classmates.

1. Above _____

_____

2. Start _____

_____

3. Every _____

_____

4. Sweep _____

_____

5. Author _____

_____

6. Teach _____

_____

7. Helps _____

_____

8. Seldom _____

_____

9. Newspaper _____

_____

10. Overpower _____

_____

27. BY THE LETTERS

Each set of letters indicates how you are to write the sentences in this activity. The words in each sentence must begin with the specific letters and in that order only. Thus, if the letters are *T t p t t n h*, the sentence could read "Take this package to the next house." Be sure to pay attention to the capital letters and punctuation. Write your sentences on the lines provided or on another sheet of paper. Good luck!

1. T i a d. _____

2. Y m r t a. _____

3. S t p i R a h. _____

4. S p a i t h n. _____

5. W t c b r? _____

6. G t r, S. _____

7. I h t g t c n. _____

8. H m c h y g t t y? _____

9. N o t w h t a. _____

10. W w w b t c c? _____

11. O c w b i t r s f t n f d. _____

12. T m w v c d t h. _____

13. S i t m i. _____

14. H w c b t t w. _____

15. T s r b A w i. _____

33

28. SENTENCES, FRAGMENTS, AND RUN-ONS

There are 6 sentences (S), 6 fragments (F), and 3 run-ons (RO) within the groups of words below. First, write the correct abbreviation on the line after the number. Then, on the appropriate line at the bottom of the page, write the two letters that follow each group of words in consecutive order. If your answers are correct, you will spell out three sentences. Good luck!

1. _____ Never in a million years. **(TH)**

2. _____ These are the facts. **(YO)**

3. _____ He spends too much money I do not spend enough. **(IM)**

4. _____ Only in your dreams. **(EB)**

5. _____ Hello. **(UL)**

6. _____ If the situation called for my help. **(AB)**

7. _____ Read the article it is very funny. **(AY)**

8. _____ You will go on the next ride with me. **(OO)**

9. _____ When the debate was over. **(YC)**

10. _____ Unless you need to talk to her immediately. **(RI)**

11. _____ Go to the desk your wallet is there. **(GO)**

12. _____ Whether you like it or not. **(ED)**

13. _____ Help me now! **(KG)**

14. _____ The dance began at eight o'clock. **(RE)**

15. _____ Robin Williams, the talented actor, starred in *Dead Poets Society*. **(AT)**

Sentences: _____

Fragments: _____

Run-ons: _____

29. SENTENCE STUFF

How well do you know sentences? Here is your chance to show your "sentence stuff"! Write the correct answers in the appropriate spaces within the crossword puzzle. Some letters have been given to help you get started.

29. SENTENCE STUFF (continued)

Across

3. sentence that contains two or more simple sentences, usually joined by a connecting word
9. two sentences joined with proper punctuation or a connecting word
10. sentence that has one subject and one verb
11. sentence that issues a command
12. punctuation mark that signals a pause
13. sentence that expresses strong feeling

Down

1. punctuation mark used at the end of interrogative sentences
2. sentence that makes a statement
3. sentence that expresses wishes or conditions contrary to fact
4. punctuation mark used at the end of declarative sentences
5. action part of the sentence that tells about the subject
6. the noun or pronoun that performs the action of the sentence
7. group of words used as a sentence although it can lack a subject, a verb, or a complete thought
8. sentence that asks a question
12. sentence that contains one independent clause and one or more dependent clauses

Section Two

PLAYING WITH WORDS

30. MAKING THE CONNECTION

How many 4-letter or longer words do you think you can make using only the letters found in this word grid? Well, we have to impose a few rules before you get started. You must spell out words that can be formed by letters that are touching each other. Thus, you can spell out *shut* since each letter touches the one that preceded it. The other rule is that you cannot stay on a letter for two turns. So, you cannot spell *cheese* because you would have to stay on the letter *e* for two consecutive turns. Other than these two, there are no rules to hold back your creativity. So get busy and, then, on a separate sheet of paper, write the words you create. Find 25 and we will be impressed!

S	E	T
K	H	A
A	C	U
R	T	E

31. JUST SAY NO!

Thirty-six words that contain the word *NO* are hidden in this word-find puzzle. The words are placed backward, forward, diagonally, and vertically. Good luck in finding the 36 hidden words.!

```
N  O  N  E  N  T  I  T  Y  N  O  X  I  O  U  S  X  T  N  B
O  G  H  S  N  D  V  N  X  S  P  M  G  R  H  H  N  Z  O  S
S  J  W  T  T  T  E  C  O  R  N  O  M  I  N  A  T  E  R  J
T  E  N  O  U  G  H  N  O  M  A  B  N  O  R  M  A  L  S  R
A  H  N  W  V  X  V  N  O  J  I  T  N  O  V  E  N  A  E  D
L  H  N  N  H  B  O  C  H  T  C  N  N  M  K  T  O  L  E  L
G  H  O  S  Q  U  K  N  L  J  E  G  A  E  G  V  O  Q  T  N
I  D  I  F  N  V  N  W  O  L  I  N  L  L  N  S  D  P  A  R
A  I  S  P  V  O  O  X  D  M  X  B  O  S  H  O  L  K  V  Z
N  G  E  R  E  H  W  O  N  M  A  N  O  R  T  H  E  S  O  N
D  N  Z  J  N  R  D  H  J  T  Y  D  O  O  M  L  V  L  N  T
M  O  V  O  B  H  B  K  O  O  C  N  N  Q  L  A  S  D  E  K
W  R  V  H  H  O  L  N  N  L  I  N  C  M  T  G  L  N  R  R
T  E  D  O  N  O  U  N  S  M  A  L  B  I  N  O  D  U  L  E
L  S  V  K  S  S  A  N  O  C  T  U  R  N  A  L  B  Q  T  C
```

ABNORMAL	NOCTURNAL	NORTH
ALBINO	NODE	NOSE
ANNOY	NODULE	NOSTALGIA
CANNOT	NOEL	NOTABLE
DENOTE	NOISE	NOUN
ENOUGH	NOMAD	NOVEL
IGNORANT	NOMINAL	NOVENA
IGNORE	NOMINATE	NOWHERE
KNOB	NONENTITY	NOXIOUS
KNOW	NOODLE	PRONOUN
MANOR	NORMAN	RENOVATE
MINOR	NORSE	SNOW

32. ONE WANTS TO HELP YOU!

One is a helpful three-letter word. Why? Well, "one" is part of each of these 25 answers. So you already have a head start knowing that "one" is in each answer. Write your answers in the correct spaces. Have fun with this one!

32. ONE WANTS TO HELP YOU! (continued)

Across

1. make up for
3. longing for friends
6. vocal or musical sound
7. single
9. past and past participle of shine
12. what David shot at Goliath
13. to improve one's skills
16. himself or herself
17. male bee
19. pennies, nickels, dimes, quarters, and such
20. hard connective tissue

Down

1. without accompaniment
2. laborious or troublesome
4. area
5. Bell's invention
8. zero
10. telling the truth
11. left
12. most immediate time
14. person very much like another
15. ice cream _____
17. finished
18. first-class (*hyphenated term*)

33. MIND YOUR P'S AND Q'S

It is very important that you mind your p's and q's today because every answer in this cross-word puzzle begins with either a *p* or a *q*. Write your answers in the appropriate spaces. Good luck!

33. MIND YOUR P'S AND Q'S (continued)

Across
1. pale
4. to form or be part of a line
5. thinking deeply or seriously
6. to make peaceful
7. still; calm
8. not fancy
9. to become enlivened
10. odd
11. capable
12. devout
13. discern

Down
1. fear
2. continue
3. interrogate
4. abandon
6. not religious; heathen
7. to repeat a passage
8. strange
9. to find fault; complain
11. to tremble or shake

34. FIND THE RIGHT SPOT!

Insert each word from Group Two into a word from Group One to form a longer word. Thus, if a Group Two word is *tar*, you can insert *tar* into a Group One word *sling* to form *starling*. Each word is used only once. Write your answers on the line next to the numerals.

Group One	
bet	show
fed	slight
import	sow
ply	sting
pure	wing

Group Two	
all	resent
heel	risk
ill	tan
leas	top
ray	wall

1. _____

2. _____

3 _____

4. _____

5. _____

6. _____

7. _____

8. _____

9. _____

10. _____

35. THE UNNEEDED LETTERS ARE NEEDED

Each of the five words in these three groups has an unneeded letter. Unscramble the letters of the 15 defined words to determine the unneeded letter. Then write that letter on the line before the numeral to spell the word that is connected to the group's title. Each word's first letter is capitalized for you. Thus, the unneeded letters are now needed letters!

Group One: What a Waste!

_____ 1. aSderit: __ __ __ __ __ __   (use ridicule or sarcasm to expose or attack vices)

_____ 2. Syarcu: __ __ __ __ __   (impertinent; rude)

_____ 3. ciToox: __ __ __ __ __   (poisonous)

_____ 4. glseGig: __ __ __ __ __ __   (type of laugh)

_____ 5. Reetscj: __ __ __ __ __ __   (to refuse to take)

The word you spelled out is _____ .

Group Two: A Real Low Point!

_____ 1. Hlbenum: __ __ __ __ __ __   (not proud; unpretentious)

_____ 2. hCasam: __ __ __ __ __   (deep breach; wide gap or rift)

_____ 3. lEaxdt: __ __ __ __ __   (to lift up with joy or pride)

_____ 4. Tidorpi: __ __ __ __ __ __   (3-legged stool)

_____ 5. ainrV: __ __ __ __   (conceited; excessively proud)

The word you spelled out is _____ .

Group Three: Break Out!

_____ 1. Veoueg: __ __ __ __ __   (fashion; accepted style)

_____ 2. peTerou: __ __ __ __ __ __   (wig)

_____ 3. lasuAt: __ __ __ __ __   (book of maps)

_____ 4. itcEvp: __ __ __ __ __   (expel by legal process; oust)

_____ 5. tyAbss: __ __ __ __ __   (bottomless, immeasurably deep space)

The word you spelled out is _____ .

36. THREE'S COMPANY

Take a three-letter combination from each column below to form a nine-letter word. For example, the "all" from Column A matches with the "otm" from Column B and the "ent" from Column C to form the word *allotment*. Write the 20 words, including *allotment*, on a separate piece of paper. Each three-letter combination is used only once.

Column A	Column B	Column C
all	anc	age
bot	ate	ate
cal	cer	cal
cha	cul	ent
con	ect	ers
dau	erw	ges
ele	est	gic
enc	gan	lal
fin	ght	ice
gem	her	ing
inv	iti	ise
mor	jud	ive
obj	otm	les
obs	our	nds
oth	rac	ned
pol	sto	nes
pre	tac	ors
str	tga	sal
tho	usa	ter
uni	ver	tly

37. THREE'S A CHARM

Today is your day to make words! Connect one part from Column A, one from Column B, and one from Column C to make a word. Each part is used only once. Write the words on the lines under the Answers column. The first one is done for you.

ANSWERS	Column A	Column B	Column C
1. _____abstract_____	ABS	AT	ABLE
2. _____	AN	ER	ACT
3. _____	COM	I	AL
4. _____	CON	IC	ATE
5. _____	DEC	LI	FEST
6. _____	EFF	LOG	HEND
7. _____	EX	OR	IENCY
8. _____	IM	PRE	IENT
9. _____	MAN	PULS	ION
10. _____	OB	QUIS	IST
11. _____	OP	TION	ITE
12. _____	PRO	TR	IVE
13. _____	PROP	VEN	OMY
14. _____	PSYCHO	VI	OUS
15. _____	RE	VIS	TY

38. HOW DO 26 LETTERS DISAPPEAR SO EASILY?

All 26 of the alphabet's letters—one per word—have been deleted. For instance, the z is missing from the first word, which is *amazing*. Remember that each letter has been deleted only once. Cross out each letter from the list below. Good luck!

a b c d e f g h i j k l m n o p q r s t u v w x y z

1. _____ amaing		14. _____ hyn	
2. _____ anoy		15. _____ maimum	
3. _____ arest		16. _____ melow	
4. _____ atest		17. _____ neighor	
5. _____ auamarine		18. _____ onderful	
6. _____ baou		19. _____ picnicing	
7. _____ bazar		20. _____ prwl	
8. _____ benin		21. _____ radi	
9. _____ elgant		22. _____ recetion	
10. _____ esence		23. _____ ridance	
11. _____ girafe		24. _____ savy	
12. _____ hiack		25. _____ vacine	
13. _____ hurra		26. _____ vacum	

39. UNSCRAMBLING THE SCRAMBLED

Unscramble the four words in each Jumble puzzle. Then unscramble the circled letters to answer each question. Enjoy!

Jumble #1

1. S E R Y L: ○ _ _ _ ○

2. P R I E G: ○ _ ○ ○ _

3. D O T N E: ○ ○ _ ○ _

4. S T B O O: _ ○ ○ _ ○

What does a bird on a seat have in common with a spy? Each is a

— — — — — — — — — — — .

Jumble #2

1. D R I E M: ○ _ _ _ ○

2. I I T O D: ○ _ _ ○ ○

3. N O C O R: _ ○ _ ○ _

4. R T E Y A: _ _ _ _ ○ ○

What is an anagram for dormitory?

— — — — — — — — —

Jumble #3

1. T E L A V: _ ○ _ ○ _

2. R T N E D: _ ○ _ _ _

3. Q L I T U: ○ ○ _ _ ○

4. R E T S S: _ ○ _ _ ○

What do 25-cent pieces and bedrooms have in common? Both are

— — — — — — — — .

Jumble #4

1. D L I I V: _ ○ _ ○ _

2. K E S E S: _ ○ _ ○ ○

3. B K S R I: ○ _ _ ○ _

4. K N O T E: _ _ ○ ○ _

What do we call President Eisenhower's motorcycles?

— — — — ʹ — — — — — —

40. A STATELY ACTIVITY

The postal abbreviations of 30 states will help you with this activity. Fill in these 30 two-letter state abbreviations to form 15 words. Each two-letter combination is used only once. The abbreviation's state is listed next to it.

1. ___ TA ___	AL (Alabama)	ME (Maine)
2. ___ ___ ANDLE	AR (Arkansas)	MI (Michigan)
3. ___ ___ ELF	CA (California)	MO (Missouri)
4. ___ L ___ NT	CO (Colorado)	MS (Mississippi)
5. ___ GU ___ NT	CT (Connecticut)	MT (Montana)
6. ___ ___ E	DE (Delaware)	ND (North Dakota)
7. ___ O ___	FL (Florida)	NE (Nebraska)
8. SE ___ ___	GA (Georgia)	NH (New Hampshire)
9. ___ N ___ R	HI (Hawaii)	OR (Oregon)
10. ___ ___ ETY	IA (Iowa)	RI (Rhode Island)
11. ___ DU ___ ION	IL (Illinois)	SC (South Carolina)
12. ___ ___ IRECT	IN (Indiana)	SD (South Dakota)
13. ___ R ___ H	KS (Kansas)	VA (Virginia)
14. ___ N ___	LA (Louisiana)	WA (Washington)
15. ___ RR ___ GE	MA (Massachusetts)	WI (Wisconsin)

41. JUMPING FROM JUMBLE TO JUMBLE

Unscramble the four words in each Jumble puzzle. Then unscramble the circled letters to complete the sentences.

Jumble #1

1. C L E I S: ◯ ◯ _ ◯ _

2. T T U N A: _ _ ◯ _ _

3. I R E E E: ◯ _ _ _ ◯

4. T S N A L: ◯ ◯ _ _ _ _

The frustrated detective was

_ _ _ _ _ _ _ _ .

Jumble #2

1. E L C H E: _ _ _ ◯ _

2. T M A L E: _ ◯ _ _ _

3. R O U S C: ◯ _ _ _ _ _

4. W N A T S: _ _ ◯ ◯ _

The workers at the mint love to make

_ _ _ _ _.

Jumble #3

1. A S E W N R: _ ◯ _ _ ◯ _

2. S F Y E T I: ◯ _ _ _ _ ◯

3. O N W D U: _ ◯ ◯ ◯ _

4. B N I R E: ◯ _ _ ◯ _

Your humerus is your _ _ _ _ _

_ _ _ _ .

Jumble #4

1. H W L A E: ◯ _ _ _ _ _

2. G E E L Y: _ _ ◯ _ _

3. B S A Y S: _ _ _ _ ◯

4. L G L E A: ◯ _ _ _ ◯

This is what the sailor saw AND felt

on the ocean blue: _ _ _ _ _ _

52

42. REPLACE TWO

Each sentence below does not make much sense because of one word. How should you make the sentence correct? First, find the word that is incorrect in the sentence and underline it. Then replace two of that word's letters with two other letters and write the correct word above the incorrect word. Thus, for the first sentence, you can see that *shirk* is incorrect. The correct word should be *shift*, a word created by replacing the letters *rk* with *ft*. The letters you are replacing do not have to be consecutive letters. Once you have made the right changes, your sentences should make more sense!

        shift
1. There was a great <u>shirk</u> in the people's opinions about the decision.

2. Some of the boaters swam to the soft near the shore.

3. Since he was so smart, he was not chosen for the basketball team.

4. She entered the room with poise and place.

5. Did you see that read of elephants cross the plains?

6. The smell of the locker containing the dirty clothes was quite ring.

7. When do they have to start the born?

8. Can you brat the brass ring on the merry-go-round now?

9. We could smell the flunk from across the country road.

10. Did the coins come up helps or tails?

11. How many charms did you and your brother have to do Saturday morning?

12. They felt really dream after the team's victory on Friday night.

13. Maybe this music will bulk the baby to sleep.

14. The blacksmith was using the angel most of the night.

15. Since Herbie could not fix the lamp, he was in a hasty mood.

43. AND COMING IN SECOND PLACE IS THE LETTER . . .

The rules are quite simple. First, you must select words that have four or more letters. Second, you must have the letter that appears next to the line as the second letter of the word you will write on the line. So, the word next to the letter *A* must have *a* as the second letter. *Lastly*, which could be your word for the letter *a*, have fun!

A. _____

B. _____

C. _____

D. _____

E. _____

F. _____

G. _____

H. _____

I. _____

J. _____

K. _____

L. _____

M. _____

N. _____

O. _____

P. _____

Q. _____

R. _____

S. _____

T. _____

U. _____

V. _____

W. _____

X. _____

Y. _____

Z. _____

44. AN ICY SITUATION

Each word below ends with ICE. Let's heat up the situation and identify these 15 words. Their definitions follow the words. Read the definitions, figure out the words, and fill in the missing letters.

1. _ _ _ ICE: to attract by offering hope of reward or pleasure

2. _ ICE: cereal grass

3. _ ICE: small cubes marked with spots

4. _ _ _ ICE: counsel

5. _ _ ICE: cost

6. _ _ _ ICE: law enforcement officials

7. _ _ _ ICE: three times

8. _ _ _ ICE: what politicians hold

9. _ _ _ _ ICE: to be enough

10. _ ICE: plural of louse

11. _ ICE: agreeable; a city in France (although the pronunciation differs)

12. _ _ ICE: spicy fragrance or aroma

13. _ ICE: small rodents

14. _ ICE: a fault or failing; in the place of

15. _ _ _ _ ICE: a home for the sick or poor

45. DAYS AND MONTHS

Listed below are 20 words containing an abbreviation for either a day of the week or a month of the year. The definition of each word is given next to each. Fill in the missing letters.

1. M O __ N   a celestial body

2. S __ U N   to daze or stupefy; shock deeply

3. W E __ D   unwanted garden growth

4. J __ A N __   pants

5. O C T __ __ __ __   sea creature with eight tentacles

6. N O V __ __   new; type of literature

7. M A R __ __ __   piece of stone sometimes used as
                          a floor covering

8. __ O C T __ __   physician

9. __ T U __ E __ __ S   those who go to school

10. F __ E B __ __   weak or infirm

11. F R I __ __ __   lively; playful; merry

12. S __ A T __   list of candidates proposed for nomination; a
                          roofing tile

13. W E __ __ D   very odd

14. A U G __ __   tool

15. F R I __ __   past tense of fry

16. M __ __ O __ N   color

17. D E C __ __ __   choose

18. W __ E __ D   to handle and use with skill and control

19. S __ A T __ __ __   smash

20. A P __ R __ __ __ __ __ __ __   near

46. ANAGRAM ALLEY

Listed below are 20 words. On the line next to each, write its anagram, the word made from rearranging its letters. In some instances, more than one anagram can be formed. The first one is done for you to help you get started.

1. coin   *icon* _____

2. keen   _____

3. mash   _____

4. shrub   _____

5. burned   _____

6. vector   _____

7. devote   _____

8. scare   _____

9. vowels   _____

10. thicken   _____

11. praised   _____

12. antlers   _____

13. slipper   _____

14. section   _____

15. senator   _____

16. terrain   _____

17. cheating   _____

18. present   _____

19. moist   _____

20. ocean   _____

47. MAKING A COMPOUND ELEMENTARY

Each word in Column A is the first part of a compound word that can be completed by correctly matching it with its second part in Column B. Write the three-letter answer from Column B next to its match in Column A. Each answer is used only once. If your answers are correct, you will spell out three famous sayings. Plus, you will make these compound words quite elementary! Write the three sayings on the back of this sheet. Good luck!

Column A		**Column B**	
1. _____ bar		king	(AIT)
2. _____ basket		self	(AN!)
3. _____ beg		stage	(ARE)
4. _____ broad		ball	(BES)
5. _____ champion		way	(DEW)
6. _____ copy		ping	(DTI)
7. _____ down		splints	(EAN)
8. _____ first		ward	(EYO)
9. _____ for		ado	(FOR)
10. _____ grand		hand	(FRE)
11. _____ home		head	(HEO)
12. _____ hot		right	(IFE)
13. _____ import		ship	(INL)
14. _____ mast		time	(NEY)
15. _____ mean		cast	(NGS)
16. _____ mocking		ever	(NOM)
17. _____ news		bird	(OUL)
18. _____ pro		paper	(OVE)
19. _____ shin		ant	(RTT)
20. _____ shop		test	(SHU)
21. _____ stair		tender	(THE)
22. _____ thin		inning	(THI)
23. _____ torn		gram	(TIM)
24. _____ what		mother	(UAL)
25. _____ your		work	(WAY)

48. THE MISSING LETTER

A letter is missing from each word below. On the short line after the misspelled word, write the letter that is left out and then write the correctly spelled word on the long line. If you are correct, your 20 consecutive letters will spell the names of four animals.

1. capaciy   ____   _____

2. artifical   ____   _____

3. forein   ____   _____

4. guarante   ____   _____

5. Febuary   ____   _____

6. inteligent   ____   _____

7. fictitous   ____   _____

8. sophmore   ____   _____

9. antena   ____   _____

10. curiculum   ____   _____

11. temperment   ____   _____

12. estacy   ____   _____

13. acount   ____   _____

14. amunt   ____   _____

15. apolgize   ____   _____

16. wining   ____   _____

17. akward   ____   _____

18. brught   ____   _____

19. alegiance   ____   _____

20. girafe   ____   _____

49. THE MISSING THREESOMES

Each word in Column A is missing a three-letter combination. Write the correct threesome from Column B in the correct space in Column A. Each threesome is used only once.

Column A	Column B
1. co _____ ge	ces
2. es _____ med	cup
3. fa _____ ue	den
4. gov _____ or	din
5. hap _____ ess	ere
6. ind _____ ment	ern
7. just _____ able	hyt
8. lo _____ le	ifi
9. neg _____ ate	mbr
10. oc _____ ant	nan
11. or _____ ary	oti
12. ref _____ nce	pin
13. reme _____ ance	sta
14. r _____ hm	spe
15. sub _____ nce	tee
16. su _____ nd	tig
17. suste _____ ce	uce
18. ten _____ cy	ura
19. uni _____ sity	vab
20. unne _____ sary	ver

50. IS IT DEADER THAN A HANGNAIL?

If you have ever heard someone say, "It is deader than a hangnail," you might have laughed. Of course, the correct word in that expression is *doornail*, not *hangnail*. Such a verbal *faux pas* (mistake) is called a malapropism, named after Mrs. Malaprop, a character in Richard Brinsley Sheridan's eighteenth-century play *The Rivals*.

Below are 20 malapropisms awaiting your editor's pen. There is at least one mistake in each statement. Cross out the error and write the correction above the statement. The first one is done for you. Good luck!

doornail
1. It was deader than a ~~hangnail.~~

2. He was a king skilled at playing the liar.

3. The government of England was a limited mockery.

4. Having two wives is called bigamy. Having one wife is called monotony.

5. Those packages were sent by partial post.

6. The inhabitants of Moscow are called Mosquitoes.

7. Indian squabs carried porpoises on their backs.

8. It is kisstomary to cuss the bride.

9. Let sleeping ducks lie.

10. The parents of Monica Green request your presents at the wedding.

11. Necessity is the mother of convention.

12. Never lift a gift horse in the house.

13. Now the shoe is on the other horse.

14. All that fritters is not gold.

15. The movie is full of interesting cartridges.

16. A rolling stone gathers no moths.

17. Socrates died from an overdose of wedlock.

18. There is no time like the pleasant.

19. You can lead a horse to water, but you can't make him think.

20. That is a horse of a different feather.

51. DID YOU WEAR YOUR CASHMERE SWEATER IN APRIL WHILE YOU DRANK CAPPUCCINO?

Cashmere, *April*, and *cappuccino* are found in this activity about word origins. Using any resources available, locate the answers to the follwing questions and circle either TRUE or FALSE. On a separate sheet of paper, write the source you used to find the answer. If your answers are correct, 10 answers are FALSE and 5 answers are TRUE. Using each number as the point value for that question, the TRUE answers total 30. Good luck!

1. TRUE or FALSE? The month *April* was named after Venus, the Roman goddess of love and beauty.

2. TRUE or FALSE? The game *badminton* was named after a type of English bird.

3. TRUE or FALSE? *Cashmere* is derived from a region of Turkey.

4. TRUE or FALSE? An *end run* is a play in football.

5. TRUE or FALSE? The word *cappuccino* comes from the religious habit worn by Italian monks.

6. TRUE or FALSE? The word *assassin* did *not* begin during the Crusades.

7. TRUE or FALSE? *Hippopotamus* was a Greek word meaning "river monkey."

8. TRUE or FALSE? *Killie* is derived from a French word meaning "to murder."

9. TRUE or FALSE? *Yoga* is originally a word from France.

10. TRUE or FALSE? *Nuke* is a diminutive of nuclear.

11. TRUE or FALSE? *Yuppie* was a term coined in the eighteenth century.

12. TRUE or FALSE? *Moron* was a character in a play by the French playwright Molière.

13. TRUE or FALSE? *Tuesday* was named after Zeus.

14. TRUE or FALSE? To *tar and feather* was originally a practical joke.

15. TRUE or FALSE? *Sirens* were originally ancient, beautiful singers.

52. GOING IN CIRCLES

At least 30 words of three or more letters are found in this circular combination of words. All the words' letters are in their correct, consecutive order, and the words are spelled in a clockwise direction. Write the words in the space at the bottom of the page.

53. START WITH IT, END WITH IT, AND ADD 3 IN BETWEEN

The directions are quite simple. Doing the activity, however, might not be so simple. Let's go slowly . . . Start with the letter given to you. End a 5-letter word with the same letter. Add three letters in between those two letters and you have completed the word. The real chore is to complete all 16 words below, so just do your best. Interestingly, six of these answers can be satisfied by using palindromes.

b __ __ __ b   l __ __ __ l

c __ __ __ c   m __ __ __ m

d __ __ __ d   n __ __ __ n

e __ __ __ e   p __ __ __ p

f __ __ __ f   r __ __ __ r

g __ __ __ g   s __ __ __ s

h __ __ __ h   t __ __ __ t

k __ __ __ k   w __ __ __ w

54. FIND THE WORDS

Here is your chance to form words one letter at a time. Start with one letter and then add another letter to it. The boxes must touch one another. You cannot stay on a letter for two consecutive turns. Thus, the word *sweet* cannot be formed, but the word *sweat* can. Each word must have at least four letters. Write the words on a separate piece of paper. Consider yourself a champion if you can form 20 words!

S	I	Z	T
S	W	E	N
M	A	R	W
H	T	O	M

55. YOUR QU IQ

An IQ test measures one's intelligence. This magic square will test your QU IQ. How? Every word in Group A contains the two-letter combination QU. Match those 16 words with their definitions by writing the corresponding number in the correct square. If your answers are correct, all the rows, columns, and the two diagonals will add up to the same number. One has been done for you.

A =	B = 15	C =	D =
E =	F =	G =	H =
I =	J =	K =	L =
M =	N =	O =	P =

Group A

A. quaint
B. quotient
C. equilateral
D. quit
E. quiz
F. require
G. inquire
H. question
I. quite
J. quotation
K. quip
L. aquamarine
M. quintuplet
N. quirk
O. queries
P. equip

Group B

1. questions
2. type of mark to indicate a person's words
3. something that is asked
4. old-fashioned in a pleasing way
5. depart from
6. short oral or written examination
7. witty or sarcastic remark
8. peculiarity
9. need
10. type of triangle
11. one of five offspring born at a single birth
12. Aries's birthstone
13. really or truly
14. to provide what is needed
15. math term
16. seek information

66

56. SS

The answer to each clue contains a *double s* combination. Thus, the answer to #4 Across is *pass*. Fill in the remaining answers and remember that each answer has *ss* as part of the word. So be *fussy* and don't make a *mess* during this *crossword* puzzle *session*!

56. SS (continued)

Across
4. football play
6. attire; a woman's piece of clothing
7. a college teacher
8. put down by force
11. state of trouble
12. tired
14. meeting
19. to give out as a task
21. voyage
23. stringy teeth cleaner
24. not neat
25. fearless

Down
1. to trouble
2. instrument that tells direction
3. more's opposite
4. push down on
5. backtalk
6. to make sad
9. emphasize
10. melt
11. special duty or function
13. evaluate
15. to give confidence to
16. picky
17. religious ceremony; amount
18. lad's female counterpart
20. ground covering
22. sheen

NAME _____ DATE _____ PERIOD _____

57. JUST DO IT!

Every one of these 28 clues shares something in common with the other clues. Each begins with the "DO" letter combination. How well you *DO* while you are *DOING* this puzzle and how well you have *DONE* altogether will only be known once this puzzle is completed. Thus, read the clues, get your pen or pencil ready, and fill in the answers. In other words, JUST DO IT!

57. JUST DO IT! (continued)

Across
1. type of film or television program
2. female deer
3. finished
4. small napkin
5. where boats land
6. tenet; belief; teachings
9. building with many rooms that are used for sleeping accommodations
10. type of singing popular during the 1950s
11. sullen or gloomy
12. having to do with the home
13. shift suddenly
15. man's best friend
16. bird that is the symbol for peace
17. American unit of currency

Down
1. contribute
2. physician
4. giver
5. small tree or shrub
6. tasty treat
7. to take one's hat off in a greeting
8. exact amount of anything, especially medicine
9. to rule or control by superior force
10. obedient
11. two-base hit
14. near the back
15. large extinct bird
16. dash's companion

58. A+ ON THESE ANALOGIES

The 16 analogies in Column A are waiting for you to match them with their counterparts in Column B. Write the correct letter in the appropriate box within the magic square. One is done for you. If your answers are correct, all rows, columns, and the two diagonals will add up to the same number—having earned you an A+ on these analogies!

A =	B = 15	C =	D =
E =	F =	G =	H =
I =	J =	K =	L =
M =	N =	O =	P =

Column A
A. soccer : goal
B. evaluate : assess
C. teacher : classroom
D. tree : leaf
E. lens : glass
F. antibiotic : infection
G. toy : yoyo
H. excerpt : book
I. alpha : omega
J. wane : moon
K. whale : pod
L. furnace : heat
M. century : year
N. water : float
O. tall : gigantic
P. duke : duchess

Column B
 1. smart : brilliant
 2. ebb : tide
 3. swatch : cloth
 4. basketball : basket
 5. wheel : spoke
 6. girder : steel
 7. kitten : litter
 8. air : glide
 9. oil: friction
10. clerk : store
11. dollar : penny
12. light : illumination
13. introduction: conclusion
14. aviator : aviatrix
15. amend: change
16. music: rap

Section Three

GETTING SET FOR THE STANDARDS

59. THE BIG AND SMALL OF IT ALL

Here is an interesting crossword puzzle. Why? Quite simply, it has no specific clues. What it does have is the idea that each answer is a word that is either a synonym for BIG or a synonym for SMALL. The first and last letters of each answer are given to you. Write your answers in the appropriate boxes. Do well!

60. FIT TO A "T"

Each of these 36 answers shares something with each other. All of them begin with the letter T. So if all of your answers are correct, you have solved this crossword puzzle and your answers are "Fit to a T"!

60. FIT TO A "T" (continued)

Across

2. allure
4. diplomatic
6. gifted
9. to bring down in football; fishing gear
10. story
11. flap
14. garment maker
18. communicate
19. printed matter
20. send
22. silent
24. entice
25. trial
26. also
27. horn

Down

1. to fall or trip
3. golf accessory
4. brown
5. instruct
6. domesticated
7. count
8. standard
9. a drink with jam and bread
10. military combat vehicle
11. writing pad
12. lofty
13. in the direction of
15. uproar
16. sharpness
17. part of a school year
18. strategy
21. constrict
23. very small
24. preposition
25. hit lightly

61. TWO CHARACTERS IN CONFLICT

Often the most intriguing parts of any literary work are the conflicts presented by the author, when one character is pitted against another. These conflicts provide interesting reading and something to think about long after you have finished reading the literary work.

    On the lines provided, answer the questions using works you have read either as class assignments or individualized readings. When you have completed your answers, share your ideas with your classmates.

1. Name a literary work that features two individuals in conflict with each other. Include the work's author and the genre. _____

_____

_____

2. Describe the conflict. _____

_____

_____

3. How did the two characters attempt to resolve the conflict? _____

_____

_____

4. To what extent were these characters successful in resolving the conflict? _____

_____

_____

5. If they were unsuccessful, what, in your opinion, contributed to their not being able to settle their differences? _____

_____

_____

6. If you had been the literary work's author, how, if at all, would you have made the outcome of this conflict different? _____

_____

_____

62. ONE VERSUS THE CROWD

An author will sometimes present one character who has a problem with those around him or her. Often these conflicts deal with philosophical differences. At times, they may even turn into physical encounters. The character who is not in agreement with the society's rules and regulations because of a basic and seemingly important difference (religious, familial, and nationalistic differences come to mind) will make the reader think carefully about the world inside (and outside) the text. After all, one of literature's purposes is to make us think. Conflicts do exactly that.

Write your responses on the lines provided. When you have finished, discuss your responses with your classmates.

1. Name a literary work that presents a conflict between an individual and his or her society.

   Include the work's author and the genre. _____

   _____

2. Describe the conflict. _____

   _____

3. How, if at all, did the character attempt to resolve the conflict with society? _____

   _____

4. Did the society make an attempt to resolve the difference(s)? _____

   _____

5. To what extent was the character successful in resolving the conflict with society? _____

   _____

6. What contributed to the conflict's resolution? _____

   _____

7. What contributed to the conflict's not being resolved? _____

   _____

63. WORKING WITH QUOTES

On many standardized English tests, you will be asked to connect a quote with a work (or two) of literature. Today you will be asked to prepare to perform such a task.

First, select one of these quotes (or the one your teacher assigns to you) and paraphrase the quote on the lines provided. Then, on another sheet of paper, tell whether you agree or disagree with the quote. Select two literary works in which the quote applies, give the title, author, and genre of each work. Finally, specifically show how the quote applies to the literary works by using concrete examples from the text. These examples can include specific quotes, characters' actions, conflicts, or any other literary techniques. Use another sheet of paper if needed.

When you have completed your writing, discuss your answers with your classmates.

"All that we do is done with an eye to something else." —ARISTOTLE

_____

_____

"Man has gone long enough, or even too long, without being man enough to face the simple truth that the trouble with man is Man." —JAMES THURBER

_____

_____

"Men can starve from a lack of self-realization as much as they can from a lack of bread." —RICHARD WRIGHT

_____

_____

"Our failings sometimes bind us to one another as closely as could virtue itself." —VAUVENARGUES

_____

_____

"The firmest friendships have been formed in mutual adversity, as iron is most strongly united by the fiercest flame." —CHARLES CALEB COLTON

_____

_____

64. MATCH THE MATE

Each word in Group A has its matching word in Group B. For example, *cloak* and *dagger* make up a matching expression, so you should place the numeral 4 in the A square. If all your answers are correct, all columns, rows, and the two diagonals will add up to the same number.

A = 4	B =	C =	D =	E =
F =	G =	H =	I =	J =
K =	L =	M =	N =	O =
P =	Q =	R =	S =	T =
U =	V =	W =	X =	Y =

Group A

A. dagger
B. forth
C. far
D. cents
E. exit
F. socks
G. bolts
H. goblins
I. blood
J. death
K. bottom
L. ladder
M. right
N. bake
O. trouble
P. games
Q. paste
R. miss
S. kicking
T. zag
U. conquer
V. ball
W. measures
X. turf
Y. ends

Group B

1. hook
2. flesh
3. hit
4. cloak
5. toil
6. divide
7. life
8. alive
9. weights
10. back
11. zig
12. bat
13. left
14. dollars
15. shoes
16. surf
17. near
18. nuts
19. fun
20. enter
21. top
22. odds
23. ghosts
24. cut
25. shake

NAME _____ DATE _____ PERIOD _____

65. ROOTING FOR YOU WITH THE ROOTS

Write the root for each word listed in the clues. Then write a different word for each root on another sheet of paper.

Across

1. short
3. bend
6. feel
8. death
10. form
12. empty
13. earth
15. great
17. hold, stretch
19. follow
20. see
22. say
23. chief, first

Down

2. conquer
4. free
5. skin
7. breathe
8. wander
9. draw, pull
11. straight
14. love
16. step
18. mind
20. build
21. flesh

82

66. MISSING-LETTER MAGIC SQUARE

Each letter in Group A has been removed from one word in Group B. Match the letter in Group A with its correct group of letters in Group B. Write your answers in the square below. One has been done for you. If your answers are correct, the columns, rows, and two diagonals will add up to the same number.

A =	B = 10	C =	D =	E =
F =	G =	H =	I =	J =
K =	L =	M =	N =	O =
P =	Q =	R =	S =	T =
U =	V =	W =	X =	Y =

Group A

A. C	M. G
B. R	N. V
C. T	O. M
D. W	P. B
E. L	Q. I
F. J	R. U
G. H	S. F
H. A	T. K
I. Y	U. Z
J. E	V. D
K. P	W. N
L. S	X. Q
	Y. O

Group B

1. attet	13. biger
2. poultr	14. beail
3. vacum	15. hiack
4. announed	16. beueath
5. imense	17. graify
6. magaine	18. myrr
7. eeri	19. terrile
8. bafle	20. reaize
9. recommed	21. hapiness
10. borow	22. ballon
11. kaya	23. bazar
12. edy	24. radi
	25. maue

67. PI

This crossword can be as easy as pie—if you remember that each answer begins with PI. So put on your thinking cap and fill in these 27 answers. Then, when you are finished, you might want to treat yourself to a piece of pie!

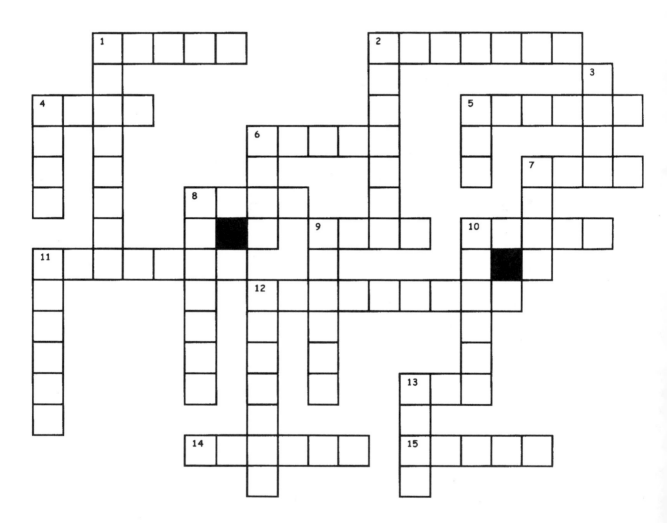

67. PI (continued)

Across
1. squeeze painfully
2. football
4. half quart
5. pleasure outing at which a meal is eaten
6. plane's controller
7. landing place for boats
8. color
9. heap
10. devotion to religious duties and practices
11. unsuspected difficulty
12. carry on the shoulders or back
13. baked dish
14. robber of ships
15. portion

Down
1. to focus on precisely; exact
2. long braid of hair
3. weapon
4. ability to feel another's suffering
5. swine
6. type of evergreen tree
7. covered with patches or spots
8. a wanderer; a traveler to a shrine
9. bird
10. vegetable
11. column
12. image or likeness
13. wind instrument

68. I SPENT THE NIGHT IN THE . . .

Twenty-five people are attending a class reunion. When asked where each spent the previous night, each person had a different response. If the first person spent the night in a bungalow, find out where the others slept by breaking the code and placing the correct letters in the correct spaces. Use the Substitution Code Helper. Since the letters J, K, Q, X, Y, and Z do not appear in any of the words in Column B, they are not included in the substitution code. After you have identified all 25, sleep well!

Column A	Column B
1. NPGVLUMT	B U N G A L O W
2. WMDBU	_ _ _ _ _
3. RMDDLVB	_ _ _ _ _ _ _
4. CIUUL	_ _ _ _ _
5. HLGAIMG	_ _ N _ _ _ N
6. DBGD	_ _ N _
7. HMDBU	_ _ _ _ _
8. RLNIG	_ _ B _ N
9. WPD	_ U _
10. RWLUBD	_ _ _ _ _ _
11. WMAFIRB	_ _ _ _ _ _ _
12. FLULRB	_ _ _ _ _ _
13. DSLIUBS	_ _ _ _ _ _ _
14. RLABDU	_ _ _ _ _ _
15. UMGVWMPAB	_ _ N _ _ _ U _ _

68. I SPENT THE NIGHT IN THE . . . (continued)

16. DBGBHBGD   _ _ N _ _ _ N _

17. IGG   _ NN

18. IVUMM   _ _ _ _ _

19. WMPABNMLD   _ _ U _ _ B _ _ _

20. DMTGWMPAB   _ _ _ N _ _ U _ _

21. EULD   _ _ _ _

22. LFLSDHBGD   _ _ _ _ _ _ _ N _

23. RMGOMHIGIPH   _ _ N _ _ _ _ N _ U _

24. DSBBWPD   _ _ _ _ _ U _

25. DBFBB   _ _ _ _ _

Substitution Code Helper

Code:	A	B	C	D	E	F	G	H	I	L	M	N	O	P	R	S	T	U	V	W
Real:	_	_	_	_	_	_	N	_	_	_	B	_	U	_	_	_	_	_	_	_

69. JAM-PACKED

These 18 words and phrases are jam-packed into this word-find puzzle. What is very convenient is that every one of them means jam-packed or tightly packed together. Circle these words and phrases that are written horizontally, diagonally, vertically, backward, and forward. Now leave yourself some room to get started! Good luck!

```
y  c  n  b  j  k  z  l  v  o  w  r  s  c  p  p  o  v  l  m
c  o  m  p  a  c  t  d  d  s  v  d  s  w  a  r  m  i  n  g
j  m  z  m  y  m  e  e  t  h  e  e  z  z  s  x  k  h  e  v
m  p  f  w  c  k  n  g  s  d  g  l  r  x  s  e  c  s  l  k
b  r  y  r  o  s  b  r  w  z  x  l  f  l  a  y  r  m  l  w
j  e  h  h  e  q  t  o  h  p  k  i  x  b  o  d  x  d  o  r
p  s  c  b  d  p  r  g  q  g  t  f  e  z  e  a  p  s  w  j
p  s  x  u  z  c  l  p  g  t  h  e  t  m  f  l  d  f  s  m
s  e  n  r  t  t  l  e  q  z  h  k  m  s  t  p  w  e  z  v
j  d  w  s  f  d  p  p  t  i  m  a  l  t  x  f  j  c  d  w
t  b  c  t  v  g  m  q  v  e  r  l  l  u  k  z  l  f  n  q
b  d  g  i  d  h  x  e  l  c  j  w  q  f  b  c  j  d  g  p
h  c  o  n  s  t  r  i  c  t  e  d  g  f  v  j  w  p  x  g
f  t  d  g  j  n  b  b  v  k  x  y  z  e  w  q  v  y  g  h
g  x  t  y  t  i  c  a  p  a  c  o  t  d  e  l  l  i  f  d
```

bursting	crowded	overloaded
choked	dense	replete
compact	filled	SRO
compressed	filled to capacity	stuffed
constricted	gorged	swarming
crammed	like a beehive	swollen

70. SHOWING WHAT YOU MEAN

First, define each noun listed below. Use your dictionary if necessary. Then, on another sheet of paper, write an illustrative sentence using the noun or a variation of it.

> **Example:** *ambivalence*: conflicting emotions toward a person or thing, as love and hate. "Juan was ambivalent about telling Martina that he wanted to break up with her."

1. guilt: _____

_____

2. concern: _____

_____

3. nostalgia: _____

_____

4. regret: _____

_____

5. fright: _____

_____

6. distress: _____

_____

7. contentment: _____

_____

8. happiness: _____

_____

9. despair: _____

_____

10. pride: _____

_____

71. KNOWING ADE IS YOUR AID

These 16 words all end with ADE. Match the definition in Column B with the correct word in Column A. Write the numbers in the appropriate squares below. One is done for you. If your answers are correct, all columns, rows, and the two diagonals will add up to the same number. Use a dictionary, if needed.

A =	B = 3	C =	D =
E =	F =	G =	H =
I =	J =	K =	L =
M =	N =	O =	P =

Column A

A. charade I. tirade
B. glade J. made
C. brocade K. lemonade
D. fade L. shade
E. grade M. trade
F. wade N. cascade
G. promenade O. parade
H. bade P. blade

Column B

1. pleaded or commanded
2. exchange; barter
3. open space in a forest
4. tasty drink
5. past tense of the verb "to make"
6. rich cloth with a raised design
7. cutting part of a tool
8. level
9. public march or display
10. walk about in shallow water
11. long, vehement speech
12. lose color
13. word or phrase acted out for others to guess
14. a trace or touch of something
15. public place for a leisurely walk
16. small, steep waterfall

72. HEAR OUR THE ERAS

This activity's title tells you much about the rest of the activity. Similar to the title, each sentence contains three mistakes. These errors can be misspellings or using incorrect words. Correct the three mistakes in each sentence by writing the correction above the mistake. The first one is done to help you get started.

threw   ball through
1. He ~~through~~ the ~~bawl threw~~ the window.

2. Wee plan too meat you later, Lesley.

3. The be smelled the sent of the beautiful garden flour.

4. When eye pushed my foot down on the car's break, I hurt my heal.

5. Has she herd watt the pour people need for the holidays?

6. Bill scraped his knee on the course bored two.

7. Whose the won who painted this pretty seen?

8. The company's quite personal director seldom waists words.

9. Wood yew change your plans if the whether turns nasty?

10. Ken has a write to right what he thinks about war and piece.

11. Their will be a miner change in the way they manufacture steal.

12. When you fined it, yews the organization's official stationary.

13. The morale of the story involves reel pane and sacrifice.

14. Her ant's favorite color is blew, and her favorite desert is vanilla ice cream.

15. Did his complement about your recent wait loss effect you?

73. FIRST AND THIRD

In each of the 20 words listed below, the first and third letters are the same. Read each word's definition and then fill in the missing letters to complete the words. Good luck!

1. A __ A __ __ __ __   (stubbornly opinionated)

2. B __ B __ __   (English officer of the law)

3. C __ C __ __ __   (desert plant)

4. D __ D __ __   (nickname for father)

5. E __ E __ __ __ __   (luxurious in a tasteful manner)

6. F __ F __ __   (seventy minus twenty)

7. G __ G __ __ __ __ __   (enormous)

8. H __ H   (exclamation)

9. I __ I __ __ __ __   (first)

10. L __ L __ __ __ __ __   (a candy)

11. M __ M __ __ __   (one who belongs to a club)

12. N __ N __ __ __ __ __ __ __ __ __ __   (one who does not go along with crowd)

13. O __ O __ __   (an unstable gas)

14. P __ P __ __   (a thin, flexible sheet made from pulp)

15. R __ R __ __ __   (uncommonness)

16. S __ S __ __ __   (a method of classification or arrangement)

17. T __ T __ __   (an appellation)

18. U __ U __ __ __ __   (small stringed instrument resembling guitar)

19. V __ V __ __   (bright or intense)

20. Y __ Y __   (child's toy)

74. A TO Z ON BOTH SIDES

Each vocabulary word in Column A has a synonym in Column B. On the line next to the Column A word, write its synonym from Column B. Each is used only once.

Column A		Column B
acme	_____	area
bastion	_____	babble
circular	_____	citadel
dagger	_____	decline
element	_____	endorsement
falsehood	_____	first
gifted	_____	gash
hazy	_____	heathen
incarcerate	_____	imprison
jolt	_____	jerk
kudos	_____	knife
lapse	_____	lie
mark	_____	misty
noise	_____	narrate
onset	_____	order
pagan	_____	pinnacle
quiver	_____	quickness
rapidity	_____	round
slay	_____	shake
tell	_____	talented
ultimatum	_____	unabridged
voluminous	_____	vessel
woeful	_____	wretched
xanthous	_____	xenon
yacht	_____	yellowish
zone	_____	zap

75. DOUBLE-LETTER DILEMMAS

The 20 sets of double letters in Column B have lost their way. Each set should be placed in its proper position within the 20 groups of letters in Column A. Each double-letter set is used only once. Write the revised spelling of each word on the line next to the letter combinations in Column A. The first one is done for you.

Column A		Column B
1. seion	*session*	aa
2. bale		bb
3. vacm		cc
4. mule		dd
5. hay		ee
6. bazr		ff
7. dale		gg
8. muer		ii
9. say		kk
10. booeeper		ll
11. haer		mm
12. ndle		nn
13. gale		oo
14. huy		pp
15. moasin		rr
16. file		ss
17. heo		tt
18. rad		uu
19. chr		vv
20. aoy		zz

76. HOW PROUD!

Take pride in your effort here. Why? The word proud appears four times as you look at the 20 four-letter words you are asked to complete. Definitions appear next to the words to help you. Fill in the missing letters and feel proud!

1. __ **P** __ __   type of stone

2. __ __ __ **R**   to burn

3. **O** __ __ __   musical composition

4. __ __ __ **U**   a color

5. __ __ **D** __   coarse or vulgar

6. **P** __ __ __   Spanish coin

7. __ __ **R** __   civil wrong

8. __ **O** __ __   dirt

9. __ __ **U** __   burden

10. **D** __ __ __   prima donna

11. **P** __ __ __   heap

12. __ __ **R**__   weaken

13. __ __ __ **O**   singer

14. __ **U** __ __   need

15. __ __ **D** __   whirlpool

16. **P** __ __ __   ashen

17. __ __ __ **R**   smell

18. __ __ __ **O**   beginner

19. __ **U** __ __   type of bed

20. __ __ __ **D**   dry

77. BOXING THEM IN

The five boxed words are looking for their synonyms. Look at the words on the next page and write the correct six synonyms for each boxed word on the lines. Each synonym is used only once. Use your dictionary, if necessary.

HONESTY	OBEDIENCE	PARDON
_____	_____	_____
_____	_____	_____
_____	_____	_____
_____	_____	_____
_____	_____	_____
_____	_____	_____

RANDOM	SMALL
_____	_____
_____	_____
_____	_____
_____	_____
_____	_____

77. BOXING THEM IN (continued)

abidance	conformity	mercifulness
acquiescence	desultory	miniscule
allegiance	diminutive	objectiveness
allowance	fairness	probity
arbitrary	haphazard	rectitude
bantam	indulgence	slender
casual	insignificant	tiny
clemency	integrity	uprightness
compliance	irregular	willy-nilly
compassion	lenience	yielding

78. OUR SPELL-CHECK IS BROKEN!

The 20 words below the word-find puzzle are all spelled incorrectly. (The numerals in parentheses indicate the number of letters in the correctly spelled words.) Yet, their correct spellings are found within the puzzle. These words are placed backward, forward, horizontally, and vertically. Circle the 20 correctly spelled words in the puzzle. Then, on a separate sheet of paper, compose a sentence for each word.

```
y  m  x  f  c  k  p  y  l  u  f  i  t  n  u  o  b  l  f
s  u  o  d  n  e  r  r  o  h  h  r  p  s  s  d  v  u  w
c  s  y  m  p  a  t  h  e  t  i  c  u  c  q  n  j  f  l
j  z  l  b  d  h  m  m  c  l  x  y  s  i  n  n  s  i  w
d  p  g  n  s  k  f  h  b  n  h  r  r  g  t  m  q  t  s
y  s  u  s  b  y  w  z  n  h  h  z  l  y  e  f  c  n  s
h  o  z  s  l  p  m  d  f  t  h  y  s  l  k  o  u  e  s
b  v  f  e  i  h  c  s  i  m  g  r  a  m  m  a  r  l  p
n  d  v  r  v  g  x  t  p  o  w  n  d  m  x  t  i  p  a
q  o  i  t  p  u  m  f  l  e  c  j  i  t  h  g  g  n  t
l  y  c  s  y  o  p  a  g  h  c  s  d  g  h  z  p  k  h
q  w  i  m  k  r  n  t  o  r  s  i  u  t  j  m  c  m  e
f  b  o  a  p  a  b  l  k  i  z  o  a  w  s  b  g  x  t
d  v  u  e  z  z  y  m  o  w  r  c  j  l  g  l  f  j  i
k  n  s  s  v  w  c  n  z  w  l  u  s  c  i  o  u  s  c
```

annalogy (7)	grammer (7)	mischef (8)	seemstress (10)
boundery (8)	horendous (10)	pathatic (8)	simpathetic (11)
bountyful (9)	lovly (6)	plentifull (9)	slite (6)
comission (10)	lusious (8)	rought (7)	speciall (7)
fruitfull (8)	mellancholy (10)	ruff (5)	visious (7)

79. GETTING INTO TOPIC SENTENCES

Decide whether each of these 15 sentences is a topic sentence or not. If it is, circle the topic and underline the opinion. If it is not a topic sentence, rewrite it (including an opinion) on another sheet of paper and make it a topic sentence.

1. Florida is one of our fifty states.

2. Smoking can be harmful to your health.

3. *Johnny Tremain* is an interesting book for seventh graders.

4. Michael Jordan is undoubtedly the world's greatest athlete.

5. Mathematics can be a difficult subject.

6. He was watching television that morning.

7. The lamp was purchased at Fred's Hardware in town.

8. Cars drive by my house.

9. Some of the officers asked the bystanders questions.

10. "Francine's" has the tastiest meals in town.

11. You are one of the friendliest people I have ever met.

12. This car is too expensive.

13. All of our beds are manufactured in this factory.

14. Kelly injured herself in the last track meet.

15. Our doctor spoke with the nurses about the situation.

80. HE AND I OR HIM AND ME?

You need to select the correct pronouns for the following 15 sentences. For example, in the sentence, "_____ went to the store," you would select "He and I" because these are nominative pronouns that act as the subject of the sentence. Circle the correct two-letter answer and then write those letters, in order, on the lines at the bottom of the page. If your answers are correct, you will spell out five words associated with cold weather.

1. The bicycle was presented to Monica by Juan and (TO) she (IC) her.

2. Kelly and (ES) he (OP) him will be at the ceremony tomorrow night.

3. The new president is (LE) she (AS) her.

4. Take the newspaper over to (DS) them (ER) they.

5. Do you know (NO) who (BE) whom will be the next senator from our state?

6. All of (WB) you (TR) youse can find the house with the help of a map.

7. One of you will be able to solve this problem by (OA) yourself (HT) yourselves.

8. (RD) Everybody (EE) All is finding the task quite enjoyable.

9. (PO) Many (IN) Much of that delicious bread was eaten by the time I arrived at the table.

10. Roberto and (GS) they (GI) them will be in the first car.

11. Send the mailings to (SE) whoever (KI) whomever you want.

12. (WE) Her (IN) She and Stan will exchange their presents after dinner.

13. Did you perform the dance by (GS) yourself (ST) youself?

14. (AR) Nobody (KA) All are going to enjoy this new movie.

15. The champions are Teresa and (TE) he (DE) him.

The five words associated with cold weather are _____

_____

_____

81. MAKING SENSE OF THESE SENTENCES

How well can you detect which is the best word to fill each blank below? For the first ten sentences, circle the correct word. For the last five sentences, the first and last letters plus the number of letters in the word are given to you. Fill in the remaining letters of the missing word. Discuss your answers with your classmates.

1. Because of the player's _____, the coach was able to play her in several positions on the basketball team.

    (A) **influence**   (B) **versatility**   (C) **flattering**   (D) **ineffectiveness**

2. Though the planners foresaw that certain problems would arise, they also found out that others were totally _____.

    (A) **impressive**   (B) **examined**   (C) **unexpected**   (D) **limited**

3. She led a rather reclusive life; as a result, _____ is known about her.

    (A) **much**   (B) **little**   (C) **mediocre**   (D) **prodigious**

4. The mediator had trouble resolving the conflict for both sides and found it hard to _____ on certain issues.

    (A) **conflict**   (B) **interpret**   (C) **founder**   (D) **compromise**

5. Michael was usually quite _____ in his efforts; many praised his outstanding work.

    (A) **ineffectual**   (B) **maudlin**   (C) **diligent**   (D) **facetious**

6. Our boss has always stressed the positive results of teamwork; thus, we tried to be as _____ as possible.

    (A) **unified**   (B) **unstructured**   (C) **prolific**   (D) **daunted**

7. The speaker was quite _____ as evidenced by the many in the audience who seemed bored and restless.

    (A) **succinct**   (B) **cursory**   (C) **verbose**   (D) **latent**

8. In the past the _____ waters of this river have been troublesome to boaters.

    (A) **placid**   (B) **turbulent**   (C) **turgid**   (D) **vapid**

81. MAKING SENSE OF THESE SENTENCES (continued)

9. The _____ he received from the critics depressed him for several months.

   (A) **ridicule**   (B) **praise**   (C) **tenacity**   (D) **apathy**

10. Even though the workers did not truly believe in the proposed changes, they were asked to _____ the ideas in public.

    (A) **scoff at**   (B) **beleaguer**   (C) **champion**   (D) **distract**

11. His s_____l (**8**) tactics were hurtful to those who had formerly known him to be kind and compassionate.

12. The cake was quite u_____e (**11**) because too little sugar had been added to it.

13. Helene seldom acted r_____y (**6**); most of the time she carefully thought about her actions.

14. The politician's fall was p_____s (**11**); only months before his popularity rating was quite high.

15. We listened to the words of the c_____r (**11**) who knew much about wines.

82. SEEING RED

Do you want a bit of help here? The 18 answers to the clues in this puzzle all begin with the word RED. (Many of the answers are two-word phrases.) Write your answers in the appropriate spaces and don't feel blue about seeing red!

82. SEEING RED (continued)

Across
1. warning of imminent danger
3. deficit or loss shown in the accounts
4. British soldier during the Revolutionary War
5. official forms and routine
6. to convert to cash
7. to lessen in any way
9. body of water between Northeast Africa and Western Arabia
10. hot enough to glow
11. small European thrush
12. to set right

Down
1. very grand or impressive welcome
2. late-night commercial airline flight
3. trick
5. to withdraw a varsity athlete
6. caught in the very commission of a crime
7. porter
8. large, sweet, bell-shaped vegetable that has fully ripened
10. giant evergreen

83. WE HAD DESSERT ON THE PLANE

This title is the only sentence in this activity that has every word spelled correctly! In each sentence below, you are to find the misspelled word and write the correct spelling on the line before the sentence. Then circle the second letter of each correctly spelled word. The first one is done for you. If your answers are correct, you have spelled the names of four world capitals.

1. a(l)lowance _____ Her mother told her to save her weekly alowance.

2. _____ The coach instilled strong disipline in all of her players.

3. _____ Several climbers found the acent up the mountain too demanding.

4. _____ Will you abreviate the names of these 20 countries?

5. _____ Our excursion's leader was almost bitten by the poisonus snake.

6. _____ Sherry is probably the most intelligant student in this group.

7. _____ His diet has made a noticable difference in his health.

8. _____ What an escipade the group experienced last night!

9. _____ My grandmother often spoke of the pleasent times she had on her aunt's farm.

10. _____ The voice teacher listened to thirty soloes on Thursday.

11. _____ Mel is a rabbid baseball fan.

12. _____ They will be encouragging us to eat a healthy diet.

13. _____ The entertainer played an instrument called a ukulile.

14. _____ Many of the students attending the assembly were moved by the paralized woman's story.

15. _____ "This is a very precius gem," stated the salesperson.

16. _____ How many hours have those dedicated scientists spent in the labortory?

17. _____ Every gymnast must be quite flexable in order to perform these challenging maneuvers.

18. _____ I found the whole scene very disterbing!

19. _____ Unfortunately, we omited his name from the program.

20. _____ We always mark those dates on the calender in our kitchen.

84. GAS AND OIL

Ready to get going? Here is some help from both gas and oil! Each answer contains either the letters GAS or OIL in that order, although there may be letters between the G-A-S and O-I-L. Fill in the answers to these clues and see where you wind up with GAS and OIL! Good luck!

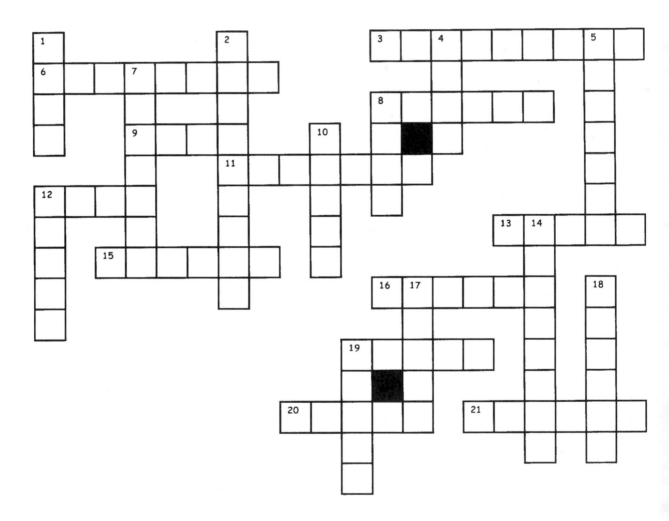

84. GAS AND OIL (continued)

Across

3. move back and forth
6. first
8. a small weakness
9. agitate
11. draw into conflict
12. dirt
13. lacey table or furniture cover
15. rubber ring placed at a joint
16. horrified
19. that which a window is made of
20. toothed wheels
21. has an annoying effect

Down

1. heat to the vaporization state
2. display rooms in a museum
4. wind into a spiral form
5. uproar
7. largest of the Great Apes
8. thwart
10. cook in the oven
12. become rotten
14. elective
17. that which lawns are made of
18. angry stares
19. hold onto tightly

Section Four

REALLY WRITING
AND REALLY DISCUSSING

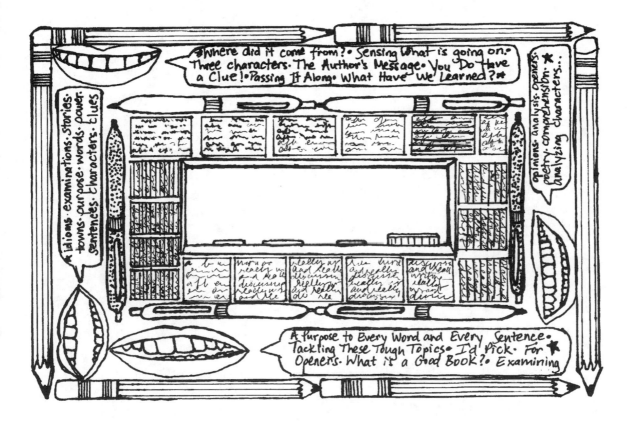

85. IDIOMS (PART ONE)

An idiom is an untranslatable expression. "To bury the hatchet," for example, means "to make peace." On a separate sheet of paper, write what you think is each expression's meaning. Then write how you think these ten idioms became part of the English language. The supposed source of each idiom is given in parentheses. Of course, there may be other supposed sources!

1. Bury the hatchet. (**Native Americans**)

2. Break the ice. (**skating**)

3. The whole nine yards. (**aircraft**)

4. Swimming upstream. (**salmon**)

5. Mind your p's and q's. (**pints and quarts**)

6. It didn't pan out. (**searching for gold**)

7. By hook or by crook. (**boating/crocheting**)

8. Saved by the bell. (**boxing**)

9. Turn over a new leaf. (**a page in a book**)

10. Barking up the wrong tree. (**hunting with hounds**)

86. IDIOMS (PART TWO)

An idiom is an untranslatable expression. For example, "to jump on the bandwagon" means to support an already popular cause or idea. On a separate sheet of paper, write what you think is the expression's meaning. Then write how you think these ten idioms became part of the English language. The supposed source of each idiom is given to you. Of course, there could be other supposed sources!

1. Jump on the bandwagon. (**baseball cancellation**)

2. Rain check. (**political campaigns**)

3. Chip on your shoulder. (**fighting**)

4. Once in a blue moon. (**two full moons in a month**)

5. On the Q.T. (**abbreviation for quiet**)

6. Red-carpet treatment. (**royalty**)

7. Get down to brass tacks. (**fabric measurement**)

8. White elephant. (**gift giving**)

9. Get into the swing of things. (**pendulum of a clock**)

10. Don't put all your eggs in one basket. (**farmers**)

87. EXAMINING EMILY

Emily Dickinson (1830–1886) is one of America's most respected (and puzzling) poets. Many of her poems have inspired great thought and discussion. Her poem "Number 315," which has been distributed by your teacher, is no exception.

First, on the appropriately numbered line, paraphrase each of the poem's 14 lines. Then the real question is "*Who* or *what* is the *He*?" in the poem. On a separate sheet of paper, answer that exact question. Give specific examples from the poem to support your opinion. Discuss your answers with your classmates.

1. _____

2. _____

3. _____

4. _____

5. _____

6. _____

7. _____

8. _____

9. _____

10. _____

11. _____

12. _____

13. _____

14. _____

88. WHAT IS A GOOD BOOK?

In an interview, Ernest Hemingway, the author of *The Old Man and the Sea*, *The Sun Also Rises*, and other novels and short stories, once said, "All good books are alike in that they are truer than if they had really happened and after you are finished reading one you will feel that all that happened to you and afterwards it all belongs to you; the good and the bad, the ecstasy, the remorse, and sorrow, the people and the places and how the weather was." On the lines provided, answer the following questions.

1. Define *ecstasy*. _____

_____   _____

2. Define *remorse*. _____

_____   _____

3. Paraphrase Hemingway's quote. _____

_____

_____

_____

_____

4. Do you agree or disagree with the quote? Why? _____

_____

_____

_____

5. Select a novel you have read and—on another sheet of paper—explain how Hemingway's quote is appropriate or inappropriate regarding that book.

6. Now that you know what Hemingway feels is a "good book," what do *you* feel is a "good book"? Write your answer on another sheet of paper.

89. WHERE DID IT COME FROM?

Have you ever thought about the origins of certain everyday expressions? Where did "lead one by the nose" or "give me five" start? How about "sitting pretty" or "in the red"?

Today is your chance to devise your own explanations of how the following ten expressions became part of our language. On a separate sheet of paper, write a paragraph on how you think each expression came into existence. Share your "story behind the expression" with your classmates. If time allows, look up the meaning and accepted story behind these expressions. How close did you and your classmates come to the real story?

1. lead by the nose

2. give me five

3. sitting pretty

4. in the red

5. hit the hay

6. salt of the earth

7. keep your ear to the ground

8. get off the hook

9. horse of a different color

10. from soup to nuts

90. TELL THE STORY BEHIND IT

Each expression below had to have a beginning, a place and time where it started. Your job is to make up "the story behind the word." On the lines following the four expressions, write your ideas as to how the expression began. Your teacher will then tell you the generally accepted story behind each expression.

1. **bite the bullet** _____

_____

_____

_____

_____

2. **back to square one** _____

_____

_____

_____

_____

3. **double-cross** _____

_____

_____

_____

_____

4. **bring home the bacon** _____

_____

_____

_____

_____

91. THREE CHARACTERS

Here are character descriptions from three different literary works. Each character is described using effective diction (word choice) and syntax (word and sentence placement). First, look up any new vocabulary words found in the three descriptions. Then circle the words that contribute to a greater understanding of each character. Lastly, on another sheet of paper, describe a character, real or fictional, using the techniques employed by Hemingway, Schaefer, or Dickens. Discuss your thoughts with your classmates.

For Whom the Bell Tolls by Ernest Hemingway

"The young man, who was tall and thin, with sun-streaked fair hair, and a wind-and-sun-burned face, who wore the sun-faded flannel shirt, a pair of peasant's trousers and rope-soled shoes, leaned over, put his arm through one of his leather pack straps and swung the heavy pack against his back. His shirt was still wet from where the pack had rested."

Shane by Jack Schaefer

"He was clean-shaven and his face was lean and hard and burned from high forehead to firm, tapering chin. His eyes seemed hooded in the shadow of the hat's brim. He came closer, and I could see that this was because the brows were drawn in a frown of fixed and habitual alertness. Beneath them the eyes were endlessly searching from side and forward, checking off every item in view, missing nothing. As I noticed this, a sudden chill, I couldn't have told why, struck through me there in the warm and open sun."

A Christmas Carol by Charles Dickens

"Oh! but he was a tight-fisted hand at the grindstone, Scrooge! A squeezing, wrenching, grasping, scraping, clutching, covetous old sinner. Hard and sharp as flint, from which no steel had ever struck out generous fire, secret, and self-contained, and solitary as an oyster. The cold within him froze his old features, nipped his pointed nose, shriveled his cheek, stiffened his gait, made his eyes red, his thin lips blue, and spoke out shrewdly in his grating voice. A frosty rime was on his head and on his eyebrows, and his wiry chin. He carried his own low temperature always about with him; he iced his office in the dog days; and didn't throw it one degree at Christmas."

92. DRAW THE DESCRIPTIONS

Here is an interesting way to "see" what authors want us to "see." First, look up any word whose definition you do not know. Then, on a plain sheet of paper, draw a picture of each character as described by the author. Discuss your drawings with your classmates.

Slake's Limbo by Felice Holman

"To begin with, Slake was small. Anyone could beat him for any reason or non-reason, and did, when they could catch him. But he was wiry and wily, too, and he could often out-run, tack, back-track, double-back, and finally dodge unseen into the subway, hiding, if possible, in some nook of the station to save the fare, or riding, if necessary, till things cooled off and the world above became habitable again. That's just to begin with."

The Scarlet Letter by Nathaniel Hawthorne

"The young woman was tall, with a figure of perfect elegance on a large scale. She had dark and abundant hair; so glossy that it threw off the sunshine with a gleam, and a face which, besides being beautiful from regularity of feature and richness of complexion, had the impressiveness belonging to a marked brow and deep black eyes. She was ladylike, too, after the manner of feminine gentility of those days; characterized by a certain state and dignity, rather than by the delicate, evanescent, and indescribable grace, (over) which is now recognized as its indication."

93. FOR OPENERS (PART ONE)

Here are the openings of three well-known novels. On the lines beneath each opening excerpt, write what you think is the author's intended purpose. Is the author establishing character? setting? conflict? Be prepared to explain your opinions. If you need additional space, use the back of this sheet.

Kidnapped by Robert Louis Stevenson

"I will begin the story of my adventure with a certain morning early in the month of June, the year of grace 1751, when I took the key for the last time out of the door of my father's house. The sun began to shine upon the summit of the hills as I went down the door; and by the time I had come as far as the manse, the blackbirds were whistling in the garden lilacs, and the mist that hung around the valley in the time of the dawn was beginning to arise and die away."

_____

_____

The Scarlet Letter by Nathaniel Hawthorne

"A throng of bearded men, in sad-colored garments and gray, steeple-crowned hats, intermixed with women, some wearing hoods, and others bareheaded, was assembled in front of a wooden edifice, the door of which was heavily timbered with oak and studded with iron spikes."

_____

_____

Bless the Beasts and Children by Glendon Swarthout

"In that place the wind prevailed. There was always sound. The throat of the canyon was hoarse with wind. It heaved through pines and passed and was collected by the cliffs. There was a phenomenon of pines in such a place. When the wind died in box canyon and in its wake the air was still and taut, the trees were not. The passing trembled in them, a sough of loss. They grieved. They seemed to mourn a memory of wind."

_____

_____

94. FOR OPENERS (PART TWO)

Here are the openings of three well-known novels. On the lines beneath each excerpt, write what you think is the author's intended purpose. Is the author establishing character? setting? conflict? Be prepared to explain your opinions. If you need additional space, use the back of this sheet.

The Crystal Cave by Mary Stewart

"I am an old man now, but then I was already past my prime when Arthur was crowned King. The years since then seem to me now more dim and faded than the earlier years, as if my life were a growing tree which burst to flower and leaf with him, and now has nothing more to do than yellow to the grave."

_____

_____

Dracula by Bram Stoker

"Jonathan Harker's Journal (kept in shorthand) 3rd May. Bistritz—left Munich at 8:35 P.M., on 1st May, arriving in Vienna early next morning; should have arrived at 6:46, but train was an hour late. Buda-Pesth seems a wonderful place, from the glimpse which I got of it from the train and the little I could walk through the streets. I feared to go very far from the station, as we arrived late and would start as near the correct time as possible."

_____

_____

The Yearling by Marjorie Kinnan Rawlings

"A column of smoke rose thin and straight from the cabin chimney. The smoke was blue where it left the red of clay. It trailed into the blue of the April sky and was no longer blue but gray. The boy Jody watched it, speculating. The fire on the kitchen hearth was dying down. His mother was hanging up pots and pans after the noon dinner. The day was Friday."

_____

_____

95. PARAPHRASING POWER

The paragraph below, excerpted from Ray Bradbury's novel *Fahrenheit 451*, contains fine examples of diction (word choice), syntax (placement of words and sentences), and imagery (images perceived by our five senses). Using these literary devices, this award-winning author certainly knows how to create vivid pictures for his readers.

Today you are asked to paraphrase (put into your own words) six sentences from the excerpt. On the lines below, using your own words, write your own version of each numbered sentence. Compare your ideas with those of your classmates.

"**(1)** The autumn leaves blew over the moonlit pavement in such a way as to make the girl who was moving there seem fixed to a sliding walk, letting the motion of the wind and the leaves carry her forward. **(2)** Her head was half bent to watch her shoes stir the circling leaves. **(3)** Her face was slender and milk-white, and in it was a kind of gentle hunger that touched over everything with tireless curiosity. **(4)** It was a look, almost, of pale surprise; the dark eyes were so fixed to the world that no move escaped them. **(5)** Her dress was white and it whispered. **(6)** He thought he almost heard the motion of her hands as she walked, and the infinitely small sound now, the white stir of her face turning when she discovered she was a moment away from a man who stood in the middle of the pavement waiting."

---

96. "FUNERAL BLUES"

Read W. H. Auden's "Funeral Blues," which has been distributed by your teacher. Then, on a separate piece of paper, answer these questions by referring to the poem.

1. Give a metaphor found in the poem.

2. Why is your answer to question 1 a metaphor?

3. Is the poem told in the first- or third-person point of view?

4. Give an example of consonance.

5. Give an example of alliteration.

6. What is the tone of the poem? (Adjectives or nouns should be given here.)

7. Give illustrative examples for question 6's answer.

8. Give an example of repetition.

9. What is the reason for the repetition?

10. What is the poem's setting?

11. What is the rhyme scheme?

12. Select a symbol and give its literal and figurative purposes.

13. How does imagery contribute to the sense and purpose of the poem?

14. Cite four examples of words whose sounds contribute to the poem's meaning.

97. THE DESERT ISLAND

It is time to ship off to that desert island, the place of quiet, comfort, and solitude. However, this desert island is a bit different from the others. It has running water, electricity, a beautiful air-conditioned house, and some other modern-day comforts. You and your family will have the entire island to yourselves for the next two months. Swimming, water skiing, and jet skiing are just some of the activites you will be able to enjoy. Sounds like fun?

Yet, there is a bit of a catch here. You are only allowed to take one of everything with you: one CD, one book, one photograph. . . . So now is the time to do some thinking about what you will pack for the trip. What you pack will tell you much about yourself.

On a separate piece of paper, write the answers to the statements below. If you choose to do so, share your answers with your classmates.

1. The CD I would take to the island is _____ because . . .

2. The book I would have with me is _____ because . . .

3. The photograph I would carry along is _____ because . . .

4. The section of the newspaper I would have delivered every day is _____ because . . .

5. The television show I would watch is _____ because . . .

6. The magazine I would have is _____ because . . .

7. The board game we would play is _____ because . . .

8. The activity I do when I am home that I would miss the *most* is _____ because . . .

9. The activity I do when I am home that I would miss the *least* is _____ because . . .

10. The videotape I would have with me is _____ because . . .

11. One of my favorite memories from home that I would often think about is _____ because . . .

12. What I would probably miss most about my home is _____ because . . .

123

98. TOWNS

Read the song lyrics distributed by your teacher. The subject matter of each song is a town. After reading the lyrics to each song, answer the following questions.

1. Each town has its problems. (A) What is a major problem with Springsteen's town? (B) What is a major problem with Allentown?

_____

_____

_____

_____

2. Cite examples of *man vs. man* conflicts in Springsteen's song.

_____

_____

_____

_____

3. Cite examples of *man vs. nature* in "Allentown."

_____

_____

_____

_____

4. How does history repeat itself in Springsteen's song?

_____

_____

_____

_____

98. TOWNS (continued)

5. Point out examples of cynicism in "Allentown."

_____

_____

_____

_____

6. How are the two songs similar?

_____

_____

_____

_____

7. How are the two songs different?

_____

_____

_____

_____

8. What images characterize Springsteen's town?

_____

_____

_____

9. What images characterize Allentown?

_____

_____

_____

99. SENSING WHAT IS GOING ON

Good writers make good use of their five senses. They allow the reader to *see*, *hear*, *taste*, *touch*, and *smell* the people, places, and things in their literary works. So, when you are reading about the beach, you can *hear* the waves, *see* the swimmers, *smell* the ocean's salt, *taste* the fried foods, and *touch* the sand. This is done, of course, through fine word choice, sentence structure, description, and imagery.

Select two of the following five scenarios. Then, on the lines, provide specific words and sensory details that you as the author would use to help your reader visualize the setting. Give at least two details per sense. For example, rather than simply stating "two people talking," write "a humorous conversation between Uncle Rich and Aunt Terry." Discuss your answers with your classmates.

A relative's house	A rock concert
A sporting event	A sleepover at a friend's house
A crowded department store	

SETTING: _____

Taste: _____

_____

Touch: _____

_____

See: _____

_____

Smell: _____

_____

Hear: _____

_____

99. SENSING WHAT IS GOING ON (continued)

SETTING: _____

Taste: _____

_____

Touch: _____

_____

See: _____

_____

Smell: _____

_____

Hear: _____

_____

100. YOU DO HAVE A CLUE!

Some people have been heard to say, "I don't have a clue!" Today will not be one of those days because you will have a clue—in fact, several clues—to help your classmates guess which of the following items you are describing.

The rules are simple. You are looking to have your partner(s) identify the object in as few verbal or written clues as possible. Each clue can have no more than three words. It cannot contain any word found in the name of the object. No hand or body motions are allowed. (This is not "Charades"!). If the object is guessed in one clue, score 1 point. If it is guessed in two clues, score 2 points, and so on. The limit is five clues. The team with the lowest number of points is the winner! Your teacher will tell you how many objects you are to describe.

airplane	charcoal grill	lamp	picture frame	stoplight
ball	cigarette	lawnmower	radio	television set
bicycle	cloud	light bulb	road	tie
blanket	coffee pot	mirror	running shoes	tire
camera	computer	mouse	scissors	tree
candlestick	cup	necklace	sidewalk	tutu
canoe	guitar	notebook	sink	wallet
cash register	jacket	oasis	spaghetti	washing machine
chalkboard	lake	photograph	staircase	window

101. THE AUTHOR'S MESSAGE

Often, your English teacher will ask you to comment on the message that a novel, play, short story, poem, or some other literary work conveys. Read the list of genres below, and think of a familiar literary title for each one. Write the title on the line provided (for example, *To Kill a Mockingbird*). Then explain what message(s) is/are conveyed by the work. Discuss your ideas with your classmates.

(1) Novel title: _____

Message(s): _____

_____

_____

(2) Play title: _____

Message(s): _____

_____

_____

(3) Short Story title: _____

Message(s): _____

_____

_____

(4) Poem title: _____

Message(s): _____

_____

_____

(5) Song title: _____

Message(s): _____

_____

_____

101. THE AUTHOR'S MESSAGE (continued)

(6) Movie title: _____

Message(s): _____

_____

_____

(7) Television Program title/episode: _____

Message(s): _____

_____

_____

(8) Newspaper Article title: _____

Message(s): _____

_____

_____

102. A PURPOSE TO EVERY WORD AND EVERY SENTENCE

Make no mistake about it—authors select their words carefully and form sentences that have a specific purpose. So when you read, digest each word and sentence (and paragraph and chapter that follows) to help you form pictures and opinions about the characters, settings, and themes in the work.

On a separate sheet of paper, in a single sentence, tell the purpose behind each paragraph below. Write the purpose in a single sentence. After you have written that sentence, support your opinion of the author's purpose with at least three specific examples from that paragraph. Share your answers with your classmates.

"A pigeon swept across her window, and she marveled at its liquid movements in the air waves. She placed her dreams on the back of the bird and fantasized that it would glide forever in the transparent silver circles until it ascended to the center of the universe and was swallowed up." (From the short story "Kiswana Browne" by Gloria Naylor)

"When Lida Mae was born the ninth of nine children, she had a 90% possibility to do and be anything she would choose. She had a good brain and disposition, good health and body, excellent looks and big legs to come in the future! She was going to be neat, petite, and all reet! As they say!" (From "Sin Leaves Scars" by J. California Cooper)

"In the 1950s many of the parishioners, seized by the national urge toward the suburbs, moved to newly integrated towns outside the city, leaving the streets around New Africa to fill with bottle and papers and loungers. The big church stood suddenly isolated. It had not been abandoned—on Sundays the front steps overflowed with members who had driven in—but there was a tentative feeling in the atmosphere of those Sunday mornings, as if through the middle of social change, the future of New Africa had become unclear." (From "New Africa" by Andrea Lee)

103. WHAT HAVE WE LEARNED?

If authors create characters to teach us more about ourselves and the world around us, what have we learned through the various literary characters we have met in our readings? Today you will have the chance to show what traits some literary characters exemplify.

Select three literary characters. For each, select any six character traits from the following lists of positive and negative personal traits. Then give an example of how the character displays each trait. Remember, you will have six examples for each character. Write your answers on a separate sheet of paper.

Positive Traits	**Negative Traits**
beautiful	deceitful
charitable	evil
classy	gluttonous
concerned	ill-tempered
famous	lazy
generous	mean
handsome	naïve
hardworking	pessimistic
honest	plotting
humorous	proud
intelligent	rude
kind	selfish
lovable	unattractive
optimistic	unintelligent
persevering	
realistic	
talented	
thoughtful	

104. WR SE QU DI

Before you think there are some major printing problems within this activity's title, do not panic. Only the first two letters of each word are given to you. So the true title should read *Writing Sentences Quite Differently*. Below are 12 sentences that are formatted the same way. On each appropriate line, write a sentence that fits this "first two letters" format. There are certainly at least several answers for each group of letters. En yo! (Enjoy yourself!)

1. Th ha al ha ma ex ti wi th fr. _____

_____

2. Wh wi yo fi th pr? _____

_____

3. He mo ca dr th bu to. _____

_____

4. Sa th la da fo hi. _____

_____

5. Ha yo se th mo ye? _____

_____

6. Br he po ba wi yo. _____

_____

7. Sh al at sp ev an mu co. _____

_____

8. Th we on tw ch th. _____

_____

9. Fo ex st wi se th cl ne we. _____

_____

10. Wh ha th an no ea ye? _____

_____

105. TACKLING THESE TOUGH TOPICS

These seven statements will inspire controversy. Circle the word AGREE or DISAGREE after each statement. Then, on the lines below the statement, write three reasons supporting your opinion. You and your classmates might want to discuss these provocative statements. Argue well!

1. Today's music influences violent behavior.   AGREE   DISAGREE

_____

_____

_____

2. Every student should be given a computer paid for by the federal government.
AGREE   DISAGREE

_____

_____

_____

3. Downloading songs from free music sites on the Internet is okay.
AGREE   DISAGREE

_____

_____

_____

_____

4. Many professional athletes and entertainers are overpaid.   AGREE   DISAGREE

_____

_____

_____

_____

105. TACKLING THESE TOUGH TOPICS (continued)

5. Capital punishment is always wrong.   AGREE   DISAGREE

_____

_____

_____

_____

_____

_____

6. The federal and state governments should pay for every citizen's medical expenses.
   AGREE   DISAGREE

_____

_____

_____

_____

_____

_____

7. People have more free time than the people who lived a century ago.
   AGREE   DISAGREE

_____

_____

_____

_____

_____

_____

106. HOW WILL IT TURN OUT?

Have you ever thought about being a screenwriter or a playwright? Well, this might be your big break. The situation, characters' names, and the first two lines are given to you. Select any one of the four situations. Then write your dialogue of at least 20 lines (10 per character) on another sheet of paper. Have fun!

Situation 1: Bob, 14, sees that his name does not appear on the list of boys selected for the school's soccer team. Immediately after, Bob knocks on the door of Coach Newsome, who has made the selections.

BOB: Coach, do you have a few minutes?

COACH: Sure, Bob, have a seat.

Situation 2: Regina, a sophomore, has made the school's cheerleading squad. Her best friend, Peggy, a junior, did not make the team. Peggy, along with Regina, had been a member of last year's team.

PEGGY: I can't believe I didn't make the team. What a jerk that coach is!

REGINA: I feel so bad for you, Peg.

Situation 3: Police Officer Jennifer Casey has stopped motorist Kevin Moore on the local highway.

CASEY: Please give me your license and registration.

MOORE: But what did I do, Officer?

Situation 4: The Freshmen Prom is a week away. Molly, Luke's date, calls Luke at home.

LUKE: Hello?

MOLLY: Hi, Luke. It's me, Molly. Um . . . I have some bad news to tell you about the prom.

107. PASSING IT ALONG

Get your pen, pencil, or computer ready. It is time to write part of the story—and then pass it along to a classmate who will write the next part. Be creative and realistic at the same time. Make the story interesting. Who knows what will happen to the story once you pass it along to another writer?

Story 1

The crowd stood in eager anticipation of what would later be called a memorable event. Television commentators, newspaper reporters, magazine writers, and others had forecasted this as a "once-in-a-lifetime event." Rachel and her two sisters, Maureen and Kate, were lucky enough to be there. And in only a few minutes, it would all begin. . . .

Story 2

Jerry Troney, a very tired housepainter, was about twenty minutes into his two-hour drive back home after completing another twelve-hour shift painting the Clefton Mansion in Inglesville. Jerry had worked these long hours for the past three weeks, and they had begun to take their toll on this sixty-year-old husband, father of two, and grandfather of six. Making his way along the dark, windy roads leading to the state highway, Jerry thought about that lingering problem. Lately, it had occupied more and more of his thoughts. He . . .

Story 3

The party had been both boring and tense. Ronnie, a fifteen-year-old girl, had not wanted to go to the party—especially since the party was held at Linda Horving's house. Ronnie and Linda had disliked each other for the past four years. Why? Nobody knew for sure, but it was quite obvious that neither girl had much respect for the other. Yet, since Ronnie's friends had talked her into going to the party, Ronnie eventually gave in. Now as Ronnie was putting on her coat ready to leave with her friends, Linda approached her and asked, "Hey, Ronnie, I'm told that you have my expensive gold watch in your coat pocket. Mind if I have a look in there now?"

108. I'D PICK . . .

You have met some interesting literary characters. Now is the time for you to see what really is important to these fictional people. Who is concerned about animals' rights? Who is into medical research? Who advocates women's rights?

On the line next to each activity, write the name of the literary character who would feel this activity is important. Be ready to support your choices. A literary character can be used more than once.

1. Feed the poor: _____

2. Cancer research: _____

3. Political action: _____

4. Animals' rights: _____

5. Women's rights: _____

6. Religious rights: _____

7. Workers' rights: _____

8. Space exploration: _____

9. Children's rights: _____

10. Civil rights: _____

Section Five

CRITICAL THINKING IS CRITICAL!

109. COMPUTERESE

Twenty terms associated with computers are hidden in this crossword puzzle. The terms are defined in the clues, but these definitions are *not* the definitions associated with computers. Thus, a *web* is defined as "that which a spider weaves." Good luck!

109. COMPUTERESE (continued)

Across

1. kind of illness that causes the common cold
4. one who makes newspaper copy
6. a bachelor's apartment
8. those who are hired to address an audience
9. development of contacts to further one's career
11. one who keeps order in the halls
12. that which a spider weaves
13. a small disc used as a fastening ornament
14. a fine-mesh object used to keep bugs from entering a home
15. that which a person says to enter a secret place

Down

2. what one can do with aluminum cans
3. that which surrounds a photograph
5. a facial cleanser containing alcohol and astringent
6. object used to stop up a hole
7. printed proof of something
8. the quickest way from one place to another
9. used to scoop fish out of the water
10. used to unlock a door
11. a tiny gray rodent
12. panes of glass

110. AS THE ANIMALS GO

Fill in the animal that is missing in each common expression below. The numeral in parentheses indicates the number of letters in the animal's name. Then circle that animal in the word-find puzzle. The words can be found forward, backward, and diagonally. Good luck!

```
B  J  L  Z  W  V  Q  B  S  L  Q  Z  B  Y  G  W  Y  B  D  Y
K  Q  N  N  Q  D  D  X  M  T  P  V  W  G  I  M  P  B  D  B
X  Y  V  Z  F  C  G  B  N  H  U  Q  S  H  R  D  B  R  Y  L
C  Q  H  S  J  R  J  N  D  Y  D  R  W  B  A  S  Q  P  T  R
D  H  N  Y  F  S  L  L  D  G  H  M  T  Q  F  H  N  V  X  K
J  U  U  L  C  T  K  M  I  W  E  D  B  L  F  D  N  A  Z  S
T  A  C  R  F  O  X  L  O  O  N  D  U  Y  E  G  O  T  I  W
P  J  V  K  C  O  N  X  L  P  N  J  L  Q  R  Q  N  G  T  L
C  V  P  R  D  H  M  H  A  X  E  S  L  B  J  A  D  X  Y  M
S  N  L  Q  V  N  M  D  M  S  D  A  N  B  H  R  N  L  B  S
D  W  L  A  R  K  J  O  B  C  B  Q  C  P  I  G  R  J  M  N
O  B  W  G  J  J  P  E  U  B  P  M  E  O  C  R  V  Z  F  M
H  G  W  F  X  D  A  K  W  S  M  L  L  N  C  S  D  B  N  Q
T  D  T  Z  D  R  Y  M  Z  Z  E  V  S  G  N  K  B  Y  Y  V
X  S  M  Q  M  T  Q  H  Z  D  D  P  Y  N  T  M  J  M  J  B
```

as a _____ takes to water (4)

as clever as a _____ (3)

as crazy as a _____ (4)

as free as a _____ (4)

as happy as a _____ (4)

as hungry as a _____ (4)

as meek as a _____ (4)

as poor as a _____ (11)

as proud as a _____ (7)

as scarce as _____'s teeth (3)

as sick as a _____ (3)

as slow as a _____ (6)

as strong as an _____ (2)

as tall as a _____ (7)

as wise as an _____ (3)

at a _____'s pace (5)

beard the _____ in his den (4)

like a _____ in a china shop (4)

the memory of an _____ (8)

the nine lives of a _____ (3)

143

111. GROUPING THEM

On the line after each foursome (or fivesome in one case), write what the group members have in common. Good luck!

1. center—linebacker—tackle—tight end: _____

2. aria—bass—contralto—soprano: _____

3. adverb—preposition—adjective—noun: _____

4. blue catfish—Chinook salmon—Nile perch—white sturgeon: _____

5. the—and—I—to—a: _____

6. Edison—Wright Brothers—Marconi—Deere: _____

7. "Love Me Tender"—"All Shook Up"—"Don't Be Cruel"—"Heartbreak Hotel": _____

_____

8. incisor—molar—bicuspid—wisdom: _____

9. 1776—1865—1929—1945: _____

10. comma—semicolon—dash—period: _____

11. poodle—beagle—setter—terrier: _____

12. ponytail—crew—bangs—permanent: _____

13. mouse—modem—DOS—RAM: _____

14. bled—set—risen—fought: _____

15. Topeka—Cheyenne—Austin—Boston: _____

112. FIGHTING A LIAR: SPOONERISMS

A spoonerism, named after Reverend William Archibald Spooner (1844–1930), is an unintentional transposition (switching) of sounds in spoken language. An example of a spoonerism is "a well-boiled icicle." Why is that a spoonerism? The speaker intended to say "a well-oiled bicycle." You could mistakenly say "I am fighting a liar" when you really wanted to say "I am lighting a fire."

Next to each spoonerism below, write what the author intended to say. Discuss your answers with your classmates.

1. Fighting a liar: _Lighting a fire_ _____

2. Ready as a stock: _____

3. You hissed my mystery lecture: _____

4. Cattle ships and bruisers: _____

5. Nosey little crook: _____

6. Our queer old dean: _____

7. We'll have the hags flung out: _____

8. You tasted two worms: _____

9. Our shoving leopard: _____

10. Is the bean dizzy?: _____

11. Go and shake a tower: _____

12. Tease my ears: _____

13. You have very mad banners: _____

14. Lack of pies: _____

15. Sealing the hick: _____

16. Go help me sod: _____

17. I'm a damp stealer: _____

18. Wave the sails: _____

19. I was chipping the flannels on the TV: _____

20. Mad bunny: _____

113. BROADWAY BOUND

Bob Bennett is Broadway bound—except for one thing. He has the names of 16 Broadway plays, but they are in "other words." Help Bob get to Broadway by correctly matching the 16 plays with their names. Write the correct numbers in the appropriate squares. One is done for you. If your answers are correct, the rows, columns, and two diagonals will add up to the same number.

A =	B = 3	C =	D =
E =	F =	G =	H =
I =	J =	K =	L =
M =	N =	O =	P =

Column A

A. *Major Barbara*
B. *Beauty and the Beast*
C. *The Lion King*
D. *The Producers*
E. *Butterflies Are Free*
F. *Unwrap Your Candy*
G. *A Thousand Clowns*
H. *Rent*
I. *Dance of Death*
J. *Chicago*
K. *The Music Man*
L. *The Women*
M. *Les Miserables*
N. *42nd Street*
O. *The Phantom of the Opera*
P. *The Sweet Smell of Success*

Column B

1. What the Landlord Expects Each Month
2. Ms. Streisand's Rank in the Armed Forces
3. The Lovely Along with the Untamed
4. 50 x 20 Funny People
5. The Home of the Bears, Cubs, Black Hawks, and White Sox
6. That Which One Imagines at the Place Where the Aria Is Performed
7. The Quite Pleasant Aroma of Winning
8. Absence of Life's Body Movement
9. Notes of the Homo Sapien
10. The Heart of New York City Theater
11. Those Who Are Very Unhappy
12. Men's Companions
13. Lepidopteran Insects Cost Nothing
14. Those Who Get Things Done
15. The King of the Jungle as the Queen's Husband
16. Take the Coverings Off the Sweets that Belong to You

114. IN OTHER WORDS

Several literary works and their authors are listed below. Select any ten. For each, invent another title in other words. Thus, *Seize the Day* could be *Carpe Diem,* and *Invisible Man* could be *Undetectable Homo Sapien.* Write your ten "in other words" titles on another sheet of paper. Then see if your classmates can guess the correct real title. Have fun!

Author	**Real Title**
1. Albert Camus	*The Stranger*
2. Kate Chopin	*The Awakening*
3. Irene Hunt	*Across Five Aprils*
4. Sharon Creech	*Walk Two Moons*
5. Gary Paulsen	*Hatchet*
6. Elie Wiesel	*Night*
7. Harper Lee	*To Kill a Mockingbird*
8. Paul Zindel	*The Pigman*
9. William Shakespeare	*The Merchant of Venice*
10. Anne Frank	*The Diary of a Young Girl*
11. S. E. Hinton	*The Outsiders*
12. J. D. Salinger	*Catcher in the Rye*
13. Jack London	*The Call of the Wild*
14. John Steinbeck	*The Pearl*
15. Robert Newton Peck	*A Day No Pigs Would Die*
16. Robert Louis Stevenson	*Treasure Island*
17. Joseph Heller	*Catch-22*
18. Ernest Hemingway	*The Sun Also Rises*
19. Bernard Malamud	*The Assistant*
20. Amy Tan	*The Joy Luck Club*
21. Alice Walker	*The Color Purple*
22. Thornton Wilder	*Our Town*
23. Richard Wright	*Native Son*
24. Jack Kerouac	*On the Road*
25. Pearl S. Buck	*The Good Earth*

115. SEEING DOUBLE

Today you will be seeing double. How? Both blanks in each sentence are to be filled in with the same word. The first blank is the person's name, and the second one is a word that is spelled the same as the name. So, if you are seeing double, you are probably seeing things the right way!

1. B_____ wanted to _____ for apples.

2. C_____ loved to sing her favorite Christmas _____.

3. Do you believe how D_____ loves to _____ those suits?

4. A_____ tried very hard in _____ class.

5. The rough current pulled E_____ into the _____.

6. F_____ is very _____ in his opinions about others.

7. G_____ might be the friendliest _____ I know.

8. I_____ gave me the _____ that she grew in her garden.

9. S_____ was forced to _____ the motorist who dented her car.

10. W_____ knew that his team could _____ the important game.

11. R_____ saw the light's _____ down the dark road.

12. V_____ read about the boxing _____ in last night's match.

13. H_____ did not _____ the smaller kids anymore after he was given detention.

14. L_____ drew beautiful pictures of the mountain _____.

15. C_____ was too much of a gentleman to be _____ with other people.

16. R_____ won the lottery and instantly became _____.

17. M_____ left his _____ on his school with all his accomplishments.

18. D_____ _____ the most humorous cartoons.

19. J_____ needed to use the car's _____ to lift the car.

20. V_____ wrote a report on the planet _____.

116. LITERARY CHARACTERS IN OTHER SETTINGS

What would Harry Potter be like as your brother, your baby sitter, or your teammate? Would Atticus Finch be a good principal or teacher? Here is your chance to see literary characters in other roles. On the lines provided, write the name of a literary character who would fit nicely into that role. Then, on another sheet of paper, write why he or she would be a good choice for that role. Use each literary character only once. Discuss your answers with your classmates.

Which character would be a good . . .

1. sister? _____

2. brother? _____

3. father? _____

4. mother? _____

5. baby sitter? _____

6. actor or actress? _____

7. medical doctor? _____

8. police officer? _____

9. neighbor? _____

10. teammate? _____

11. teen counselor? _____

12. principal? _____

13. boss? _____

14. friend? _____

15. class president? _____

117. SOUNDS LIKE A PROVERB BUT . . .

Each of these crazy groups of words sounds somewhat like a proverb. Write the correct proverb on the appropriate line. You might want to say each one aloud—but not too loudly!—to help you identify each proverb. One is done for you.

1. Cuties lonely thin Jeep.   _Beauty's only skin deep._ _____

2. Bold rabbits by yard.   _____

3. Bobbing reader due bay ball.   _____

4. Go boozes hood booze.   _____

5. Lever took a rift course inner south.   _____

6. Let her save then saw he.   _____

7. Men he ands make right lurk.   _____

8. Bet creeping logs sigh.   _____

9. Late binds stink a bike.   _____

10. Awls bare inn coven wore.   _____

11. Demands roam tis is vassal.   _____

12. So instead he wins to pace.   _____

13. Being is relieving.   _____

14. Malls of years.   _____

15. Dime lures tall dings.   _____

16. Will daughter funs leap.   _____

17. Bare the sod end foil the piled.   _____

18. Learn Dee udder seek.   _____

19. Lad ooze gravels last.   _____

20. Might mire whiff mire.   _____

118. A MIXED-UP WORLD

Suppose you woke up one morning and the following changes had taken place overnight. Write three specific effects for each change. An example is done for you. Discuss your answers with your classmates.

> **Example**: *You are a foot taller!* (a) I would have to buy new clothes.
> (b) I might be able to dunk a basketball. (c) I could date taller people.

1. *Mirrors do not exist.*

(a) _____

(b) _____

(c) _____

2. *Twenty-four-hour cameras have been placed in every classroom.*

(a) _____

(b) _____

(c) _____

3. *You have a third eye—in the back of your head.*

(a) _____

(b) _____

(c) _____

4. *Computers in your country only work for the same two hours (7 to 9 P.M. Eastern Standard Time) each day.*

(a) _____

(b) _____

(c) _____

118. A MIXED-UP WORLD (continued)

5. *Each family can fill up the family's cars with gas only once a week.*

(a) _____

(b) _____

(c) _____

6. *You have moved 300 miles away.*

(a) _____

(b) _____

(c) _____

7. *Media, including newspapers, television, and radio, have been shut down for the next two weeks.*

(a) _____

(b) _____

(c) _____

8. *Your two best friends have moved three towns away.*

(a) _____

(b) _____

(c) _____

9. *A board of very conservative public officials has banned any song lyrics the board members deem controversial.*

(a) _____

(b) _____

(c) _____

10. *People speak in monosyllabic words only.*

(a) _____

(b) _____

(c) _____

119. LUCKY 13

For many people, 13 is an unlucky number. Yet, today, 13 is the best number. Why? Because 13 is the highest point value for any word.

In this game, you will list words and score the number of points according to how many letters are in the word. So, if you list a seven-letter word, you score 7 points. Today, the highest you can score is 13. So 13 is not unlucky—it is the best you can be!

The following is an example. On a separate sheet of paper, write the numerals from 1 through 13 and then list your words. Then calculate your score by adding the words' values. A perfect score is 91 points. Do your best!

Example:

1. A

2. AT

3. DIN

4. CART

5. DIRTH

6. MEANER

7. SEVERAL

8. LIFELIKE

9. STRUCTURE

10. IMPEDIMENT

11. ABANDONMENT

12. THEMATICALLY

13. SPASMODICALLY

Score: _91_

120. FIND THE FOUR AND SCORE

The letters in Column A have been substituted for the real letters in Column B. So each time you see a *W* in Column A, it is really a *Q*. Each time you see an *M*, it is really a *U*. Fill in the blanks in Column B, using the Code Helper below. For each word you identify, score 1 point. Write your score beneath Column B.

Column A (Substitute letters)	Column B (Real letters)	Column A (Substitute letters)	Column B (Real letters)
1. WMCN	Q U __ __	14. NZAE	__ __ __ __
2. BCXB	K __ __ K	15. OCTV	__ __ __ __
3. CQXY	__ __ __ __	16. PAEI	__ __ __ __
4. DMOS	__ U __ __	17. GQRJ	__ __ __ __
5. ESZT	__ __ __ __	18. RXYZ	__ __ __ __
6. FRBZ	__ __ K __	19. SLRJ	__ __ __ __
7. AMCT	__ U __ __	20. TMBZ	__ U K __
8. HARJ	__ __ __ __	21. MAPZ	U __ __ __
9. UEQZ	__ __ __ __	22. VMGQ	__ U __ __
10. JRIT	__ __ __ __	23. AZGQ	__ __ __ __
11. KCTV	__ __ __ __	24. XEEB	__ __ __ K
12. LELL	__ __ __ __	25. YCAZ	__ __ __ __
13. QRLB	__ __ __ K		Score _____

Code Helper			
Sub:	__ K __ __ __ __ __ __ __ __ __ __ __ U __ __ __ __ __ __ __ __ __ Q __ __ __
Real:	A B C D E F G H I J K L M N O P Q R S T U V W X Y Z

121. CAUSE AND EFFECT

Each statement below purports to contain a cause-and-effect relationship. Identify each statement as one of the following and write the letter on the line:

A. True cause and effect
B. Necessary condition, not cause

C. Reversing cause and effect
D. Coincidence

_____ 1. Reports of criminal activity tend to increase when there is a full moon. The full moon must impact on people's behavior.

_____ 2. The only reason the United States was able to maintain its independence was because it had abundant natural resources.

_____ 3. There is a severe drought in the Northwest that has caused many forest fires.

_____ 4. For the last five years, the team with the highest payroll has won the World Series. So, if we pay our team's players more money, we'll win the World Series.

_____ 5. Whenever I have a cold, I take Vitamin C and within 10 days the cold goes away. Vitamin C is a cure for colds.

_____ 6. Every time I drink regular coffee before I go to bed, I have trouble sleeping. The caffeine must keep me awake.

_____ 7. Every time the assistant principal comes to our volleyball game, we win. She brings us good luck.

_____ 8. Ninety-five percent of all cocaine addicts drank alcohol before they were legally permitted to do so. Early alcohol use leads to cocaine use.

_____ 9. People who live in Florida live longer on average than those who live in the Northeast. So, if I move to Florida, I will live longer.

_____ 10. I have problems with my satellite TV reception whenever there are thunderstorms in my area. The thunderstorms are the cause of the poor reception.

122. NOT JUST THE FACTS

Identify each of the following statements as FACT, GENERALIZATION, INFERENCE, OPINION, or some COMBINATION.

1. Jason is the best athlete in the school.

   _____

2. Most truck drivers have tattoos.

   _____

3. Before Alaska and Hawaii, the last two states to join the union were Arizona and New Mexico.

   _____

4. A large number of African-Americans have made important contributions to the music industry.

   _____

5. Barbara not only gets low grades, but she also disrupts the other students.

   _____

6. He wouldn't look me in the eye, so I knew he was not telling the truth.

   _____

7. After he wrote *The Catcher in the Rye*, J. D. Salinger became very reclusive.

   _____

8. Samantha won the election by 300 votes.

   _____

9. Mr. and Mrs. DeAngelo are very happily married.

   _____

10. It is cold in February.

   _____

123. JUST BECAUSE

Each statement below contains a conclusion and some evidence to support that conclusion. Just because evidence is being offered, is it convincing? Why? Why not? Write your comments on another sheet of paper and discuss them with classmates.

1. Dr. Jones is an excellent laser eye surgeon. A number of prominent celebrities have endorsed his work.

2. No one has been able to disprove that there is life on other planets, so it stands to reason that there must be.

3. It seems obvious that Mr. Smith didn't commit the crime with which he is charged, because there was not enough evidence to convict him.

4. Transvision makes the best television in America. Their brand is owned by more people than any other brand.

5. Despite the fact that changing the traffic patterns around the park will result in increased congestion, the idea that we can plant more trees and shrubs, and make it look like it did when we were children, makes this the right thing to do.

6. State Senator Lawlor is the best candidate running this year. Besides, if he isn't reelected, a number of my close friends will be out of jobs.

7. This development project is not good for the city. Why, just two years ago the city council voted against it, and now they want to reconsider it.

8. This proposal to reduce homelessness has no merit; after all, it is being advanced by this "fringe" group—Citizens for a Safer City.

9. I don't think the new highway superintendent is very well respected. I have not heard of anyone who has made any positive comments about him.

10. We have no right to criticize human rights' violations in other countries. Look at the way our country has treated certain groups of people.

124. LOGIC PROBLEMS

Here are four logic problems for you to solve. Work out your answers on a separate piece of paper and write your answers under each problem. Think well!

1. Alan, Bob, and Casey are members of the football team. The quarterback has never missed a practice. Casey is taller than the quarterback. Bob couldn't practice for a week after he injured his hand on the halfback's helmet. **Of the three positions—tight end, halfback, and quarterback—which ones do Alan, Bob, and Casey play?**

_____

2. Christine is a teacher, Alexis is a doctor, and Ellen is a stockbroker. They are dating three male friends—Ted, Joe, and Bill. Alexis is going out with Ted's best friend. Christine has not met Joe, and Alexis introduced Joe's date to him. **Who is going out with whom?**

_____

3. Four members of the gymnastics team—Aaron, Barry, Chuck, and Dave—competed in four events—floor exercise, rings, parallel bars, and horse. The judges gave scores of 6.0–10.0 in gradations of tenths. Each athlete won an event outright—there were no ties. **Who won each event?** (1) In the event that Dave won, he scored a perfect 10. (2) Barry and Chuck earned the same score in the floor exercise. (3) Barry scored higher on the horse than Aaron got on rings. (4) The winning score in rings and parallel bars were the same. (5) Chuck earned a tenth of a point less on rings than Dave got on the horse. (6) Dave did poorly in the floor exercise.

_____

4. Bob, Jim, and Frank, and each of their twin sisters—Amy, Mary, and Kristen—are seniors at the same high school. **Who are brother and sister?** (1) Bob is a good athlete and used to be on the student council. (2) During Period 4 Jim and his sister are in the same classroom adjacent to the one Amy is in. (3) Frank's sister is on the student council with Mary. (4) Amy is a good athlete who plays three sports. (5) Mary's brother is always the first person at Period 5 lunch because the classroom he is in prior to that is the only classroom close to the cafeteria. (6) Kristen does not care for sports, but she sometimes goes to watch Bob's games.

_____

125. IT'S ALL IN THE NAME

For each category below, select a name. For each letter of that name, list one word that describes or has something to do with that person, place, or thing. An example is given. Discuss your answers with your classmates.

---

scientist: EDISON—E (electricity) **D** (determined) **I** (intelligent) **S** (scientific)
O (original) **N** (novel)

---

1. **classmate:** _____

_____

2. **television character:** _____

_____

3. **literary character:** _____

_____

4. **city or town:** _____

_____

5. **recording group:** _____

_____

6. **toy:** _____

_____

7. **automobile:** _____

_____

8. **movie:** _____

_____

125. IT'S ALL IN THE NAME (continued)

9. **historical figure:** _____

_____

10. **athlete:** _____

_____

11. **season of the year:** _____

_____

12. **actor or actress:** _____

_____

13. **vacation spot:** _____

_____

14. **sport:** _____

_____

15. **musical instrument:** _____

_____

126. R U O-K?

Today you will learn to read in a whole new way. Your eyes and ears will help you figure out each sentence or question below. Sound out the letters in each group of words. If there is a hyphen between letters, say or blend those letters together. Thus, this activity's title asks, "Are you okay?" Write your version of the following groups of words.

1. D X-M S E-Z. _____

2. D-S S D Q-R. _____

3. U-R D 1, J. _____

4. N-E-1 C R-T? _____

5. I M 2 B-Z 4 U. _____

6. Y R U D-Z? _____

7. U R A Q-T, L-X! _____

8. E S X-M-N-N D I-S. _____

9. D B S D N-M-E. _____

10. S M-T, D! _____

11. S D-S X-T-C? _____

12. D-T S 4 U. _____

13. C D B-D I-S? _____

14. I K-N W, N-R-E. _____

15. D B-S-KT-S R 4 U. _____

127. HELP!

You will help yourself in this activity appropriately entitled "Help." All the words in the Real Letters column are synonyms for the word *help*. You must figure out what letters from the Code Letters column were substituted for the real letters. For example, the code letter *R* is the real letter *O*; the code letter *N* is the real letter *L*; and the code letter *O* is the real letter *C*. Substitute the appropriate letters and place them in the Letter Substitution Code at the bottom of the page. Now help yourself to these 20 words!

	Code Letters	Real Letters
1.	SEIU	__ __ __ __
2.	ERRLU	__ O O __ __
3.	FAII	__ __ __ __
4.	ESOM	__ __ C __
5.	ISLI	__ __ __ __
6.	SPK	__ __ __
7.	LGLUSPV	__ __ __ __ __ __ __
8.	RENPZI	O __ L __ __ __
9.	LGOORA	__ __ C C O __
10.	FSBRA	__ __ __ O __
11.	IVDSVOI	__ __ __ __ __ C __
12.	SLLPLU	__ __ __ __ __ __
13.	AILOGI	__ __ __ C __ __
14.	LGCCRAU	__ __ __ __ O __ __
15.	ORVUAPEGUI	CO __ __ __ __ __ __ __
16.	LGELPKPHI	__ __ __ __ __ __ __ __ __
17.	IVKRALI	__ __ __ O __ __ __
18.	LSVOUPRV	__ __ __ __ __ __ O __
19.	SOORTTRKSUI	__ CCO__ __ O __ __ __ __
20.	ORNNSERASUI	COLL __ __ O __ __ __ __

Letter Substitution Code

Code: A B C D E F G H I K L M N O P R S T U V Z

Real: __ __ __ __ __ __ __ __ __ __ __ __ L C __ O __ __ __ __ __

128. WONDERING WHAT IT MEANS

Here are ten letter combinations. Notice we did not say they are words. Let's pretend for a little while, however, that they are words. On the lines following each word, write: (A) How is the word pronounced? Use your own method. (B) What does the word mean? (C) Why does the word mean that to you? There are no absolutely correct answers, so your answers will be accepted; just have some sensible reason why you gave the answers you did. An example is given. Compare your answers with those of your classmates.

---

droltene:

(A) *"droll teen"* _____

(B) *It is a type of cough medicine.* _____

(C) *The "drol" sounds medicinal. The "tene" sounds as if it is a chemical.* _____

---

1. **lytork:**

   (A) _____

   (B) _____

   (C) _____

2. **dostifical:**

   (A) _____

   (B) _____

   (C) _____

3. **cambino:**

   (A) _____

   (B) _____

   (C) _____

4. **physteeny:**

   (A) _____

   (B) _____

   (C) _____

128. WONDERING WHAT IT MEANS (continued)

5. **thixy:**

   (A) _____

   (B) _____

   (C) _____

6. **swosp:**

   (A) _____

   (B) _____

   (C) _____

7. **shondue:**

   (A) _____

   (B) _____

   (C) _____

8. **oprichette:**

   (A) _____

   (B) _____

   (C) _____

9. **dopexx:**

   (A) _____

   (B) _____

   (C) _____

10. **zipnorf:**

   (A) _____

   (B) _____

   (C) _____

129. ALLITERATIVE SLOGANS

Today you can make-believe you are working for an advertising agency. Your sole responsibility is to create slogans for different companies; however, there is a catch. Each slogan must be alliterative! So, Joe's Car Wash could be "Champion Car Cleaners" and Springfield's Hotel could be "Your Home Away from Home." Here's your chance to be creative! You may either write your slogans on another sheet of paper OR design the slogans using colored markers or pencils. Have fun!

1. Robinson's Law Firm

2. Antiques-R-Us

3. Franklin's Office Supplies

4. Laura's Music Lyrics

5. Natural Beauty Fences

6. Laser Printer Repair Company

7. Martin Brothers Moving Company

8. Roy's Insect Exterminators

9. Rowland's Rubbish Removal

10. Boulder Creek Home Builders

11. Webster's Pool Installation

12. Around-the-Clock Plumbers

13. Terry's Florists

14. Saint Rose's Medical Center

15. Family Landscapers

130. RHYMING YOUR TIME AWAY

Each phrase below has a two-word rhyming equivalent. Thus, if the clue is "uncontrollable youngster," "wild child" is an appropriate answer because the two words rhyme. Put on your thinking cap and write your answers on the appropriate lines. Good luck!

1. husbands' mates' cutting devices   _____

2. intrepid serf   _____

3. humorous dough   _____

4. deafening horde   _____

5. ill candle tip   _____

6. odd couple   _____

7. baseball pitcher's area   _____

8. President Hoover's ices   _____

9. Ms. Pitcher's cable cars   _____

10. Warsaw resident's acting gigs   _____

11. Ringo's containers   _____

12. South American mountain range's sweets   _____

13. William's cash registers   _____

14. asp's deceptions   _____

15. thankful father   _____

16. Jefferson's vows   _____

17. shouts from the pig's home   _____

18. initial need for water   _____

19. terrific spouse   _____

20. Michael's preferences   _____

131. ALL IN A LINE NOW!

Match the words in Column A with the words in Column B to form 21 compound words. Write each two-letter answer from Column B next to its appropriate partner in Column A. Each answer is used only once. If your answers are correct, you will spell out a sentence that is directly related to this activity's title!

Column A		Column B	
1. _____ air		**(AR)**	edge
2. _____ back		**(AS)**	stand
3. _____ black		**(EI)**	smith
4. _____ candle		**(EL)**	ship
5. _____ down		**(EN)**	proof
6. _____ dust		**(ES)**	shirt
7. _____ elbow		**(ET)**	lock
8. _____ foot		**(EU)**	stab
9. _____ friend		**(IL)**	foot
10. _____ grand		**(OS)**	ball
11. _____ head		**(OU)**	way
12. _____ high		**(QU)**	port
13. _____ mast		**(RD)**	pan
14. _____ pad		**(RL)**	head
15. _____ pocket		**(RS)**	bank
16. _____ river		**(SA)**	stick
17. _____ straight		**(T!)**	bench
18. _____ sweat		**(TE)**	book
19. _____ tender		**(TF)**	line
20. _____ weather		**(WH)**	room
21. _____ work		**(WO)**	town

132. THINKING CRITICALLY WITH WORDS

Find what is common to each of the five words in each group below. The commonality has nothing to do with meaning, but it could have much to do with the formation of their letters or what could be added to each word in the group. Write your answers on the lines below the groups.

1. **grave, lime, tomb, touch, whet**

_____

_____

2. **kayak, level, noon, racecar, radar**

_____

_____

3. **annual, cycle, plane, pod, weekly**

_____

_____

4. **race, read, region, room, rose**

_____

_____

5. **babble, poppy, mommy, sassafras, tatter**

_____

_____

6. **absolute, effigy, ghost, hire, stall**

_____

_____

7. **clad, frog, jerk, maroon, sport**

_____

_____

133. MORE THINKING CRITICALLY WITH WORDS

Find what is common to each of the five words in each group below. The commonality has nothing to do with meaning, but it could have much to do with the formation of their letters or what could be added to each word in the group. Write your answers on the lines below the groups.

1. **lease, narrow, queue, rogue, though**

_____

_____

2. **age, art, bound, mind, thought**

_____

_____

3. **bazaar, melee, radii, taboo, vacuum**

_____

_____

4. **gull, lions, port, shore, son**

_____

_____

5. **dazzle, devil, grudge, long, take**

_____

_____

6. **braids, doors, fries, toast, vanilla**

_____

_____

Section Six

RESEARCHING AND REMEMBERING

134. AND WHERE DID THIS ONE COME FROM? (PART ONE)

Today you will display your talent in research and word origins. How? Just match the words in Column A with their origins in Column B. Write the proper number in each box. One is done for you. If your answers are correct, all the rows, columns, and the two diagonals will add up to the same number.

A =	**B =** 3	**C =**	**D =**
E =	**F =**	**G =**	**H =**
I =	**J =**	**K =**	**L =**
M =	**N =**	**O =**	**P =**

Column A
A. carnival
B. February
C. Frisbee
D. dreadlocks
E. curfew
F. bedlam
G. bikini
H. cashmere
I. babble
J. bonfire
K. guillotine
L. Atlas
M. caterpillar
N. dandelion
O. cappuccino
P. easel

Column B
1. a region of northern India
2. a celebration of the flesh
3. the goddess of fertility
4. atomic bomb testing on a Pacific Ocean island
5. people's bones burned in an outdoor fire
6. religious garb of French monks
7. donkey
8. Biblical story about a tower
9. a humane doctor
10. lion's tooth
11. a hairy cat
12. a Titan who had to hold the pillars supporting the heavens
13. times to cover the fire
14. Ethiopian warriors
15. a Connecticut bakery
16. a London insane asylum

135. AND WHERE DID THIS ONE COME FROM? (PART TWO)

Show off your talents for word origins today! Match the words in Column A with their origins in Column B. Write the proper number in each box. One is done for you. If your answers are correct, all the rows, columns, and the two diagonals will add up to the same number.

A =	B = 13	C =	D =
E =	F =	G =	H =
I =	J =	K =	L =
M =	N =	O =	P =

Column A

A. marathon
B. hypocrite
C. hick
D. hippopotamus
E. ladybug
F. March
G. hopscotch
H. hulk
I. jeopardy
J. husky
K. piggyback
L. migraine
M. lunatic
N. jinx
O. maverick
P. Motown

Column B

1. a cattle owner
2. river horse
3. Eskimo
4. the Blessed Mother
5. a chess term
6. a god of agriculture and war
7. the car manufacturing industry in Detroit
8. rural towns
9. an unwieldy ship
10. a pack or bundle
11. an ancient Athenian war victory
12. a southeastern United States bird
13. an ancient Greek actor
14. the moon
15. the Scottish word for "score"
16. words meaning "half" and "cranium"

136. AND WHERE DID THIS ONE COME FROM? (PART THREE)

Today you will display your talent in research and word origins. How? Just match the 16 words in Column A with their origins in Column B. Write the proper number in each box. One is done for you. If your answers are correct, all the rows, columns, and the two diagonals will add up to the same number.

A =	**B =** 13	**C =**	**D =**
E =	**F =**	**G =**	**H =**
I =	**J =**	**K =**	**L =**
M =	**N =**	**O =**	**P =**

Column A
A. robot
B. slipshod
C. stewardess
D. trivia
E. potluck
F. sniper
G. poll
H. siren
I. tarantula
J. salary
K. smog
L. September
M. sandwich
N. sideburns
O. rugby
P. zany

Column B
1. a school in England
2. where three roads met
3. part of a Roman soldier's pay
4. whatever was left in the cooking pot
5. a city in southern Italy
6. a bird
7. Italian theater character
8. a keeper of the pigs
9. beautiful daughter of the ancient Greek sea god
10. combining "smoke" and "fog"
11. a play by Karel Capek
12. a Union general during the Civil War
13. footwear originally created for indoor use only
14. a marathon gambling session
15. the word for "head"
16. Latin word for "seven"

137. FAMOUS YOUNG PEOPLE

Sixteen people who were famous when young, some real and some fictional, have been gathered to see how well you know who they are. Match each famous young person in Column A with the area in Column B in which he or she gained fame. Write the correct number in each box. One is done for you. If your answers are correct, all rows, columns, and the two diagonals will add up to the same number.

A =	B = 15	C =	D =
E =	F =	G =	H =
I =	J =	K =	L =
M =	N =	O =	P =

Column A
A. Sarah Hughes
B. Tom Sawyer
C. Chelsea Clinton
D. Le Ann Rimes
E. Nadia Comaneci
F. Holden Caulfield
G. Mary Shelley
H. Stevie Wonder
I. Dorothy Gale
J. Lucy
K. Harry Potter
L. Wendy Darling
M. Pollyanna
N. Charlie Brown
O. Helen Keller
P. Elvis Presley

Column B
1. Gold-Medal skater
2. male comics character
3. female comics character
4. Gold-Medal gymnast
5. author
6. J. M. Barrie's creation
7. sang "Love Me Tender"
8. former White House resident
9. writer/lecturer although blind and deaf from infancy
10. female singer of Country music
11. his song entitled "Fingertips" went to #1
12. J. K. Rawling's fictional boy
13. fictional Kansas farm girl
14. Salinger teen
15. Mark Twain's creation
16. the ever-optimistic fictional girl

138. AWARD-WINNING MUSICIANS

Match each recording artist in Column A with the award-winning song in Column B. Write your answers in the magic square below. One is done for you. If your answers are correct, all columns, rows, and the two diagonals will add up to the same number.

A =	B = 2	C =	D =	E =
F =	G =	H =	I =	J =
K =	L =	M =	N =	O =
P =	Q =	R =	S =	T =
U =	V =	W =	X =	Y =

138. AWARD-WINNING MUSICIANS (continued)

Column A

A. Bette Midler
B. Enya
C. Billy Joel
D. Santana
E. Michael Jackson
F. Roberta Flack
G. Christopher Cross
H. Carole King
I. Whitney Houston
J. Tony Bennett
K. U2
L. The Eagles
M. Sheryl Crow
N. Tina Turner
O. Eric Clapton
P. Phil Collins
Q. Simon and Garfunkel
R. Frank Sinatra
S. Celine Dion
T. Toto
U. Bobby Darin
V. Percy Faith
W. USA for Africa
X. Herb Alpert
Y. Seal

Column B

1. "A Taste of Honey"
2. "Only Time"
3. "I Left My Heart in San Francisco"
4. "All I Want to Do"
5. "Another Day in Paradise"
6. "Wind Beneath My Wings"
7. "I Will Always Love You"
8. "Hotel California"
9. "Rosanna"
10. "We Are the World"
11. "Mrs. Robinson"
12. "Kiss from a Rose"
13. "Just the Way You Are"
14. "Killing Me Softly With His Song"
15. "What's Love Got to Do With It"
16. "It's Too Late"
17. "Beautiful Day"
18. "My Heart Will Go On"
19. "Theme from *A Summer Place*"
20. "Beat It"
21. "Change the World"
22. "Strangers in the Night"
23. "Mack the Knife"
24. "Smooth"
25. "Sailing"

139. LOOK IT UP (ROUND ONE)

Very simply, the game is called *Look It Up*. Each answer is worth 5 points as you work your way toward 100 points. Research skills, patience, and perseverance are essential. When you have found the correct answer, write it in the space after the question. Your teacher will establish how much time is allowed for all 20 questions. After your teacher gives you the answers, write the number of points you have earned at the bottom of this page. Try hard as you "look it up."

1. Joseph Conrad, author of *Heart of Darkness*, was born in what country?

2. What Massachusetts town was the home of poet Emily Dickinson?

3. Who is Agatha Christie's egotistical Belgian detective?

4. Who created Pooh Bear?

5. Who was King Arthur's wife?

6. What French king said, "I am the state"?

7. What was Dickens's last novel, unfinished at his death?

8. Who was Jane Eyre's love?

9. What British novelist was born in Iran in 1919 and brought up on a farm in Zimbabwe?

10. In which European city would one find the Bridge of Sighs?

11. Who painted *Falling Rocket: Nocturne in Black and Gold?*

12. Which aviator flew the *Spirit of St. Louis*?

13. What is the study of medical problems associated with the aged?

14. In what five-letter word do you hear only the first letter?

15. Who is the supreme god of Hinduism?

16. What literary character sold his soul to the devil?

17. Who created that loveable cartoon canine Snoopy?

18. How many people serve on a U.S. petty jury?

19. Which is larger in area—Texas or Spain?

20. Where is the Sea of Tranquillity?

Score: _____ points

140. LOOK IT UP (ROUND TWO)

Each answer in round two of *Look It Up* is worth 5 points. Research the following 20 questions, and then write the correct answer to each one in the space after the question. When your teacher gives you the answers, write your score in the appropriate space at the bottom of the page

1. What war began in 1950?

2. In 1821, Brazil gained its independence from what nation?

3. Who was known as "The Lady with the Lamp"? She lived from 1820–1910.

4. How many legs does a spider have?

5. Do birds or mammals have hotter body temperatures?

6. How often are Nobel Prizes awarded?

7. Where did explorer Ferdinand Magellan die?

8. New Delhi is what country's capital?

9. Who wrote the poem "Ulysses"?

10. What sport features the shuttlecock?

11. Who had a record album entitled *Cold Spring Harbor*?

12. How many lines are in a sonnet?

13. Tom Brokaw is associated with what television network?

14. The fictional Joad family is from which U.S. state?

15. Which of the 26 letters is used most frequently in the English alphabet?

16. Dr. James Naismith invented which sport?

17. Which fun board game can be translated as "one many"?

18. How old was Albert Einstein when he formulated his special theory of relativity in 1905?

19. John Lennon, Paul McCartney, Ringo Starr, and George Harrison were The Beatles. What was the name of the group McCartney formed after The Beatles broke up?

20. In what city and state is Mark Twain buried?

Score: _____ points

141. CHALLENGING QUOTATIONS

If you set your mind to it, finding the answers to these ten quotations is not as difficult as it may first appear. There are clues in many questions to help you identify the answer. Use any source you want. Write the answer on the appropriate line. Then discuss with classmates the sources you used.

1. Name the English scientist who wrote in a 1675 letter, "If I have seen further it is by standing on the shoulders of giants." His initials are I.N. _____

2. The following quote is excerpted from which 1962 film? "I was to think of these days many times. Of Jem and Dill and Boo Radley and Tom Robinson—and Atticus."

_____

3. Which early 20th century U.S. President had promised a "chicken in every pot"?

_____

4. Which philosopher and author, whose initials are G.S., once said, "Those who cannot remember the past are condemned to repeat it"? _____

5. After the Battle of Zela in 47 B.C., Julius Caesar said, "I came, I saw, I conquered." What is the Latin translation of this quote? Circle one: **(A)** Vici, Vidi, Veni.   **(B)** Veni, Vici, Vidi.
(C) Veni, Vidi, Vici.

6. Name the American author, who was born in 1835 and died in 1910, who said, "I came in with Halley's Comet in 1835. It is coming again next year, and I expect to go out with it."

_____

7. Before she was beheaded in 1536, who allegedly said, "The executioner is, I hear, very expert and my neck is very slender"? _____

8. Which Daphne du Maurier novel opens with the line "Last night I dreamt I went to Manderley again"? _____

9. Whose second half of the 20th-century Inaugural Address included the following words: "Let every nation know . . . that we shall pay any price, bear any burden, meet any hardship, support any friend, oppose any foe to assure the survival and success of liberty"?

_____

10. Which ill-fated future U.S. President once said, "The ballot is stronger than the bullet"?

_____

142. CAN YOU FIND IT?

Fifteen answers are waiting for you to find them. Using any available research tools, locate the correct answer and write it on the line following the question. Then discuss with classmates the sources you used. Good luck!

1. _____ Who was the baseball 1997 National League Most Valuable Player?

2. _____ In what state did Mariah Carey attend high school?

3. _____ What is Italy's monetary unit?

4. _____ What was the maiden name of William Shakespeare's wife?

5. _____ Who was President Harry Truman's successor?

6. _____ Where is your bicuspid located?

7. _____ Who was the director of E.T.?

8. _____ Is a "greenback" a plant, money, or a seasoning?

9. _____ Who coined the word "nerd"?

10. _____ Where did the Lego toy originate?

11. _____ In the year 2000, the world's population was approximately how many billion people?

12. _____ What does the musical term "lento" mean?

13. _____ A "ground stroke" is associated with which sport—football, polo, or tennis?

14. _____ Charles Dickens wrote during which century?

15. _____ What distance is a furlong?

143. THE RESEARCH PROVES IT

Your research talents will be put to the test in this activity. Twenty-five clues from a range of subjects need answers. Do your proper research and match the clues in Column A with their proper answers in Column B. Write your answers in the magic squares below. One is done for you. If you are correct, all columns, rows, and the two diagonals will add up to the same number.

A =	B = 10	C =	D =	E =
F =	G =	H =	I =	J =
K =	L =	M =	N =	O =
P =	Q =	R =	S =	T =
U =	V =	W =	X =	Y =

143. THE RESEARCH PROVES IT (continued)

Column A

A. 1966
B. Aesop
C. CT
D. Victoria
E. Yiddish
F. Chicago
G. Kennedy
H. Dodgson
I. Australia
J. France
K. Macbeth
L. angels
M. Franklin
N. Lincoln
O. Band
P. Woodstock
Q. moon
R. Freud
S. Fulton
T. Cohan
U. golf
V. pyramids
W. Massachusetts
X. Clinton
Y. Andy

Column B

1. the year the Miranda decision was handed down by the Supreme Court
2. the only state carried by George McGovern in 1972
3. "Yankee Doodle Dandy" was about this composer
4. "Fools rush in where _____ fear to tread"
5. the natural home of the Tasmanian Devil
6. Socks and Buddy were this U.S. President's pets
7. 1969 music festival
8. inventor of the bifocal
9. Joan of Arc's country
10. fablist who coined the phrase "slow and steady wins the race"
11. writer Lewis Carroll's real last name
12. "Mensch" originated in this language
13. only surviving wonder of the Seven Wonders of the Ancient World
14. inventor of the steamboat
15. supposed unlucky Shakespearean play
16. the word "lunacy" is derived from this celestial body
17. said, "A house divided against itself cannot stand"
18. Rennie Davis, Tom Hayden, Abbie Hoffman, and Jerry Rubin are forever associated with this Midwest American city
19. abbreviation of the state where the Frisbee™ was first popularized
20. the first name of the artist Warhol
21. the B in a CB radio
22. U.S. President associated with the Bay of Pigs invasion
23. British queen who reigned for more than 60 years
24. sport associated with rounds and links
25. the id, ego, and superego psychoanalyst

TEACHER PAGE FOR ACTIVITY 144, TOPICS

This game asks the students to think of answers that are appropriate to the information contained in the rows and columns. If the row (horizontal) is *5-letter verbs* and the column (vertical) is *B*, an appropriate answer is *begin*. If the row is *European cities* and the column is *L*, an appropriate answer is *London*. The students should try to fill in as many boxes as they can.

Some suggestions for this game are as follows:

1. The topics and letters can be selected by either you and/or your students. Topics that your students have covered are certainly a priority, especially if you are using this game as a review for an exam. If not, select other topics.

2. It is suggested that the less frequently used letters of the alphabet—*Q, X,* and *Z*—be avoided as column headers. Selecting words beginning with those letters, though not impossible, can be difficult.

3. Decide how long you want to allow the students to work before you call time.

4. If only one student or group has the correct answer, score 3 points. If more than one share the answer, score 1 point. Total the points after you and the students have gone over their written responses.

5. How this game is played will often depend upon the number of students in your class. Each student should try to find an answer for each box. If you feel that going around and listening to 25 answers (if that is the number of students in the class) for each box will take too long, you might want to ask the students to form small groups and decide what is the best answer for each box. They can then use that one answer as their group's choice.

144. TOPICS

Your teacher will tell you what letters to write above each column and what topics to write next to each row. Fill in the square with a good answer. If you are the only one with that appropriate answer, score 3 points. If you and any other(s) have the answer, score 1 point.

145. FAMOUS PEOPLE

Quite possibly, you might know who many of these famous people are. If you do not, why not consult a book, a friend, a relative, or the Internet? Match each person in Column A with the field in Column B in which he or she gained fame. Write the correct number in each appropriate box. One is done for you. If your answers are correct, all columns, rows, and the two diagonals will add up to the same number. Good luck!

A =	B = 3	C =	D =
E =	F =	G =	H =
I =	J =	K =	L =
M =	N =	O =	P =

Column A

A. exploration
B. film
C. music
D. computers
E. religion
F. poetry
G. art
H. architecture
I. physics
J. social work
K. politics
L. theater
M. botany
N. astronomy
O. medicine
P. psychology

Column B

1. Niccolo Pisano
2. George Washington Carver
3. Federico Fellini
4. Spiro Agnew
5. Lillian Wald
6. Beverly Sills
7. Alfred Binet
8. John Harvard
9. Elizabeth Blackwell
10. Gwendolyn Brooks
11. Gabriel Fahrenheit
12. Bill Gates
13. Hernando de Soto
14. Lope de Vega
15. Grandma Moses
16. Johannes Kepler

146. LOUIE IS LOST!

Poor Louie. He made big plans for a great summer road trip, but there is one problem. Louie is lost! He was not given the names of the 16 cities he was going to visit. Instead, he was given only their nicknames. Help Louie find his way by correctly matching the city in Column A with its nickname in Column B. Write the correct letter next to its appropriate number within the box. One is done for you. If your answers are correct, all the columns, rows, and the two diagonals will add up to the same number.

A =	B = 6	C =	D =
E =	F =	G =	H =
I =	J =	K =	L =
M =	N =	O =	P =

Colulmn A

A. Philadelphia
B. Los Angeles
C. New York City
D. Denver
E. Atlanta
F. Birmingham
G. Minneapolis/
   St. Paul
H. Detroit

I. Pittsburgh
J. St. Louis
K. Dallas
L. Boston
M. Chicago
N. Washington,
   D.C.
O. New Orleans
P. San Francisco

Colulmn B

1. The Pittsburgh
   of the South
2. The Steel City
3. The Big Easy
4. The Mile-High City
5. The Windy City
6. The City of Angels
7. The Motor City
8. The Big D

9. The Big Apple
10. The Golden Gate City
11. The Gateway to
    the West
12. The Dogwood City
13. Bean Town
14. The Twin Cities
15. The City of
    Brotherly Love
16. The Nation's Capital

147. THE TYPES OF READING MATERIALS

Here are 15 different types of reading materials or genres in Column A. Match each one to its example(s) in Column B by writing the correct letter on the line in Column A. Each answer is used only once.

Column A

1. _____ epic

2. _____ autobiography

3. _____ bibliography

4. _____ short story

5. _____ atlas

6. _____ textbook

7. _____ anthology

8. _____ biography

9. _____ periodical

10. _____ novel

11. _____ journal

12. _____ essay

13. _____ manual

14. _____ play

15. _____ almanac

Column B

A. the story of your life written by yourself

B. a book that includes *A Raisin in the Sun*, "The Necklace," and "The Raven"

C. "The Ransom of Red Chief" by O. Henry

D. *Rent*, *Hamlet*, and *Romeo and Juliet*

E. a person's account of his or her daily events

F. *The Outsiders* and *The Adventures of Tom Sawyer*

G. countries' maps and geographical terms of the world

H. Homer's *The Odyssey*

I. list of books to read if you wanted to learn more about a subject or topic

J. book used by physics students

K. *Time* or *Newsweek*

L. an article showing the writer's thoughts on why the government should lower the voting age

M. information about weather, celebrities, countries, sports, etc.

N. a book explaining how to build a shed for your backyard

O. the story of George W. Bush's life as written by another person

148. YOU AND YOUR SURROUNDINGS

It is time to take a hard look at yourself and the places and things around you. You can use any sources you choose. Books, the Internet, and relatives are some suggestions. Write your findings on the appropriate lines. (Use another sheet of paper if you need more space for your answers.)

1. How did your town get its name? _____

_____

2. How did your school get its name? _____

_____

3. What is the meaning of your first name? _____

_____

4. What is the meaning of your last name? _____

_____

5. What is the meaning of your state's or province's name? _____

_____

6. What is your country's motto? Why is that an appropriate motto? _____

_____

7. What is your country's symbol? Why is it an appropriate symbol? _____

_____

8. Why does a local professional sports team have the name it does? _____

_____

149. ADD THEM UP!

Add up the numbers associated with each of the words or prefixes in these 15 equations. You will need to do some research for several of the answers. Write your answers on the appropriate line.

1. trio + quad + number of days in a fortnight = _____

2. mono + di + penta = _____

3. oct + nona + deca = _____

4. quad + hept + number of years in a score + uni = _____

5. number of years in a century + quint + nonagon = _____

6. decade + hex + millennium = _____

7. penta + decathlon + fourscore = _____

8. triad + quad + deca = _____

9. quad + penta + century = _____

10. mono + score + decade = _____

11. number of Amendments in the Bill of Rights + White House address on Pennsylvania Avenue = _____

12. number of members of the U.S. Congress + deca = _____

13. number of U.S. states + number of letters in England's capital city = _____

14. the Bicentennial year of the United States + oct + decade = _____

15. famous London address on Downing Street + novena + tetra = _____

150. DO YOU KNOW THE U.S.?

Here are 20 statements and questions about the United States. First, see how many you can complete without looking up any information. Then, using whatever resources you need, answer the remaining questions. Write each correct letter on the line next to the question. If your answers are correct, you will spell out a famous U.S. landmark and its location. Write the famous landmark and its location on the line after question 20.

1. _____ The largest state is **(S)** Texas **(T)** Alaska **(U)** California.

2. _____ The smallest state is **(H)** Rhode Island **(I)** Idaho **(J)** Delaware.

3. _____ The highest mountain is **(C)** Mount Washington **(D)** Mount Marcy **(E)** Mount McKinley.

4. _____ The state having the longest coastline is **(S)** Alaska **(T)** California **(U)** Maine.

5. _____ The geographic center of the 48 contiguous states is in **(D)** Oklahoma **(E)** Kansas **(F)** Missouri.

6. _____ *Dakota* is a Sioux word for **(A)** friend **(B)** river **(C)** plains.

7. _____ The famous Appomattox Court House is in the state of **(P)** Illinois **(Q)** West Virginia **(R)** Virginia.

8. _____ Where is Devils Tower? **(R)** Arkansas **(S)** Wyoming **(T)** Tennessee

9. _____ Who was the only president to serve more than two terms? **(T)** Franklin Roosevelt **(U)** Ronald Reagan **(V)** Harry Truman

10. _____ Martin Van Buren is buried in **(M)** Massachusetts **(N)** Ohio **(O)** New York.

11. _____ The Jimmy Carter Library is in **(W)** Georgia **(X)** Mississippi **(Y)** Connecticut.

12. _____ President Lyndon Johnson's wife's nickname is **(D)** Bess **(E)** Lady Bird **(F)** Lamb.

13. _____ Hillary Rodham Clinton graduated from what college? **(Q)** Bowdoin College **(R)** Wellesley College **(S)** Princeton University

150. DO YOU KNOW THE U.S.? (continued)

14. _____ Who wrote the words of "The Star-Spangled Banner"?   **(A)** Betsy Ross
(B) Harriet Raleigh   **(C)** Francis Scott Key

15. _____ The motto of the United States is   **(G)** The Proud and the Many
(H) In God We Trust   **(I)** All for One and One for All.

16. _____ Who wrote the poem "The New Colossus" that appears on the pedestal below the
Statue of Liberty?   **(I)** Emma Lazarus   **(J)** Emily Dickinson   **(K)** Walt Whitman

17. _____ What is the last word of the song "America, the Beautiful"?   **(C)** sea
(D) land   **(E)** law

18. _____ **(A)** James Buchanan   **(B)** Abraham Lincoln   **(C)** Andrew Johnson was the 15th
president.

19. _____ The state in which the greatest number of presidents were born is   **(F)** Ohio
(G) Virginia   **(H)** Massachusetts.

20. _____ Who is the only president so far who had never married?   **(M)** Herbert Hoover
(N) Franklin Pierce   **(O)** James Buchanan

The famous U.S. landmark and its location:

_____

151. REALLY RESEARCHING

Here is your chance to complete this crossword puzzle—after you have completed your research! Look up anything you don't already know. Then fill in the correct answers in the appropriate spaces and you will be a winner!

151. REALLY RESEARCHING (continued)

Across

3. first name of artist Gainsborough
4. state where Wallingford is located
5. won Grammy Award for Best Album in 1997
7. famous golfer Tiger
8. baseball player called "the Yankee Clipper"
11. boxer called "The Greatest"
13. voted Best Picture of 1997
14. founded Microsoft
15. North Atlantic _____ Organization
16. politician assassinated in Dallas in 1963
17. sang "Are You Lonesome Tonight?"

Down

1. the original James Bond
2. first U.S. astronaut to orbit the Earth
3. capital of Libya
4. impeached in 1998
5. newspaper, *The Wall Street* _____
6. first player to break the color barrier in baseball
9. St. Louis Cardinal who hit 70 homers
10. sport of Snead, Palmer, and Ballesteros
11. official language of Lebanon
12. Last name of Malcolm X

152. WHAT A YEAR!

Though there is a very good chance many people do not remember some of the events of 1987, an interesting year, you can help them along with your research. Match each item in Column A with its counterpart in Column B.

Column A

1. _____ centennial

2. _____ New York Giants

3. _____ Iran-Contra

4. _____ Alysheba

5. _____ Mikhail Gorbachev

6. _____ Oprah Winfrey

7. _____ James Baldwin

8. _____ Marlee Matlin

9. _____ Minnesota Twins

10. _____ Ronald Reagan

11. _____ Corazon Aquino

12. _____ Jesse Jackson

13. _____ *Fences*

14. _____ Edmonton Oilers

15. _____ Black Monday

16. _____ *Platoon*

Column B

A. Stanley Cup winners

B. Kentucky Derby winner

C. Best Picture at the Oscars

D. World Series winner

E. big political affair

F. August Wilson play starring James Earl Jones and Mary Alice

G. leader of the Philippines

H. Super Bowl champions

I. talk show host who won two daytime Emmy Awards

J. Soviet leader

K. 46-year-old Baptist minister who was a U.S. presidential candidate

L. was the U.S. president

M. won the Oscar for Best Actress in *Children of a Lesser God*

N. Hollywood celebrated its _____ birthday

O. terrible day for the U.S. stock market

P. *Notes of a Native Son* author who died in December

153. THE MISSING LINK

Match the words in Column A with their missing links in Column B. Write your answers in the magic square below. One is done for you. If your answers are correct, all columns, rows, and the two diagonals will add up to the same number.

A =	B = 10	C =	D =	E =
F =	G =	H =	I =	J =
K =	L =	M =	N =	O =
P =	Q =	R =	S =	T =
U =	V =	W =	X =	Y =

153. THE MISSING LINK (continued)

Column A

A. sea

B. ours

C. first

D. foremost

E. *Newsweek*

F. jelly

G. happiness

H. q's

I. Brahms

J. rail

K. handsome

L. justice

M. Eve

N. matter

O. brawn

P. barrel

Q. steady

R. dimes

S. night

T. Becky Thatcher

U. cream

V. deliver

W. span

X. golden

Y. countrymen

Column B

1. " . . . with liberty and _____ for all."

2. Beethoven, Bach, and _____

3. nickels and _____

4. "One if by land, two if by _____"

5. brains and _____

6. coffee and _____

7. road and _____

8. day and _____

9. spic and _____

10. yours, mine, and _____

11. Tom Sawyer and _____

12. stand and _____

13. Adam and _____

14. first and _____

15. peanut butter and _____

16. "Silence is _____."

17. " . . . and the last shall be _____."

18. " . . . life, liberty, and the pursuit of _____."

19. lock, stock, and _____

20. *Time* and _____

21. tall, dark, and _____

22. "Friends, Romans, and _____ . . ."

23. p's and _____

24. slow and _____ wins the race

25. mind over _____

154. WOMEN WRITERS

The first names of 16 women writers are in Group A. Match them up with the correct 16 last names in Group B by writing the correct number in the appropriate box within the Magic Square. If your answers are correct, all columns, rows, and the two diagonals will add up to the same number.

GROUP A

A. Margaret
B. Judy
C. Anne
D. Sylvia

E. Lillian
F. Toni
G. Gloria
H. Willa

I. Fannie
J. Emily
K. Sue
L. Shirley

M. Gwendolyn
N. Edith
O. Zora
P. Alice

GROUP B

1. Bradstreet
2. Dickinson
3. Morrison
4. Hurston

5. Walker
6. Hellman
7. Flagg
8. Plath

9. Brooks
10. Cather
11. Jackson
12. Mitchell

13. Blume
14. Grafton
15. Naylor
16. Wharton

A =	B = 13	C =	D =
E =	F =	G =	H =
I =	J =	K =	L =
M =	N =	O =	P =

155. LITERARY HUNT

The following questions from the field of literature are waiting for you to answer them. How you locate the answers is up to you. Write your responses in the space next to the questions. Then discuss with classmates the sources you used.

1. Which William Blake poem begins with the line "Tiger! Tiger! Burning bright"?

2. Who wrote the poem beginning with these lines: "I'm Nobody! Who are you? Are you—Nobody—too?"

3. Which novel is closest to being Charles Dickens's autobiography?

4. Who was Sherlock Holmes's loyal companion?

5. Who wrote *The Yearling*?

6. Who wrote the Harry Potter series?

7. How many lines are in a sonnet?

8. How many syllables are in a haiku poem?

9. What state provides most of the setting for *An American Tragedy* by Theodore Dreiser?

10. What was Saki's real name?

11. What playwright wrote *Hay Fever* and *Private Lives*?

12. What poet is famous for his poems written primarily in lower-case letters?

156. BY THE NUMBERS

Here is your chance to show your knowledge of numbers. Write the correct numbers in their proper places within the magic square. All the first words have been purposely left in lower-case letters. If your answers are correct, the rows, columns, and two diagonals will add up to the same number. If necessary, use research books and other sources to help you solve this magic square. Good luck!

A =	B = 22	C =	D =	E =
F =	G =	H =	I =	J =
K =	L =	M =	N =	O =
P =	Q =	R =	S =	T =
U =	V =	W =	X =	Y =

156. BY THE NUMBERS (continued)

Column A

A. fifteen

B. twenty

C. twelve

D. sixty-four

E. nine

F. thirty

G. fourteen

H. twenty-three

I. thousand

J. thirteen

K. five

L. eleven

M. eighty-seven

N. seventy-six

O. fifteen

P. three

Q. one

R. ten

S. four

T. thirty-one

U. eight

V. two

W. one hundred

X. seventeen

Y. seven

Column B

1. number of years in a century

2. movie and book: *The* ____ *Musketeers*

3. number of trombones that led the big parade in *The Music Man*

4. ____ lines in a sonnet

5. ____ angles in a nonagon

6. number of days in December

7. number of years mentioned in Lincoln's "Gettysburg Address"

8. number of days in April

9. Shakespeare was born in fifteen ____

10. Shakespeare's ____ *Gentlemen of Verona*

11. numbers of combined events in a decathlon and a pentathlon

12. ____ syllables in a haiku poem

13. movie and book: ____ *Flew Over the Cuckoo's Nest*

14. number of minutes in an NFL quarter

15. Michael Jordan's uniform number with the Chicago Bulls

16. the number seven's lucky companion

17. thought to be an unlucky number

18. "____ Days of Christmas"

19. movie: ____ *Men Out*

20. number of seasons in the calendar year

21. movie: *A* ____ *Clowns*

22. number of years in a score

23. ____ Wonders of the Ancient World

24. book and movie: ____ *Little Indians*

25. movie: ____ *Easy Pieces*

Section Seven

YOU ARE SPECIAL

157. YOU AND A FRIEND

How well do you know yourself? How well does a friend know you? How well do you know that friend? These questions will probably be answered as you do this activity.

First, answer each question on the appropriate line. Then partner up with a friend. Review each question together and share your responses. If a response is too personal, you do not have to share that information. Your friend will probably correctly guess some of your answers. Others, perhaps, will be too personal or too old for him or her to know. Did your friend anticipate your answers? Did you do the same for your friend? Lastly, select one of your responses and expand it into a well-written paragraph using correct grammar and punctuation. Write that paragraph on a separate sheet of paper. Have fun!

1. Because I love _____ (type of food) so much, I would find it hard to give it up for a long time.

2. I feel one of my most attractive qualities is _____.

3. A friend's parent whom I admire is _____

_____.

4. A recent news story that really interested me was _____

_____.

5. One question that I would like to ask my English teacher is _____

_____.

6. When I turn 40 years old, I would like to be working as a(n) _____

_____.

7. A frightening thing that happened to me was _____

_____.

8. What I enjoy most about school is _____

_____.

9. A magazine I like is _____.

10. A television show I really enjoy is _____.

158. WHAT DO YOUR ANSWERS TELL YOU?

On a separate sheet of paper, answer these ten questions by listing at least three reasons why you feel the way you do. Then, read through your responses and list five things you have learned about yourself from those responses. You might want to share your answers with your classmates.

1. Are you more like a snow-capped mountain or a white, sandy beach?

2. Would you rather produce a popular CD or be given a modeling contract?

3. Would you rather own a luxurious New York City apartment or the world's most luxurious sports car?

4. In the future, would you rather be a member of the winning World Series team or own a profitable technology company?

5. Would you rather spend a month helping the poor in a Third-World country or spend a month at your grandparents' home or apartment?

6. Do you think you are more like a stoplight at a busy intersection or a dust storm in the plains?

7. Would you rather be the host of a popular television game show or be the all-time prize-winning player on that same game show?

8. Are you more like a well-written essay, a humorous play, or an emotional song?

9. Are you more like a Monday morning, a Friday night, or a Sunday afternoon?

10. Do you more resemble a lion, a puppy, a wolf, or a monkey in temperament?

159. CONNECTING YOUR THOUGHTS

Start with any word that is appropriate for the topic. The next word must begin with the last letter of the previous word. Take the topic "Positive personal characteristics" as an example. If the word you begin with is *truthful*, you can then use *loving*, then *generous*, then *smart*, then *tactful*, followed by *likable*, *energetic*, *classy*, *youthful*, and *learned*.

For each topic below, list a minimum of ten words. Write your responses on a separate sheet of paper.

Topic # 1: Animals

Topic # 2: Verbs

Topic # 3: Items in a supermarket

Topic # 4: 5-letter words

Topic # 5: Famous people's last names

Topic # 6: Words having at least five letters including two vowels

Topic # 7: Things you see in a major city

Topic # 8: Words that function as at least two parts of speech

Topic # 9: Things associated with winter

Topic #10: Foods

160. A WAY WITH WORDS

Include these 15 words, in order, in your story and you have done your job. The story can be about anything—serious, humorous, happy, sad, or anything else you want. You are the author of this story. Your teacher will tell you what story or stories to do. Write or type your story on a separate sheet of paper.

Story #1	Story #2	Story #3	Story #4
advance	celebrate	agent	bench
approach	drop	aging	bothered
back	extend	career	cemetery
continue	finish	compensate	different
controlled	include	compete	especially
heart	like	dramatic	former
jumping	nearly	earned	foul
mention	potential	great	future
nervous	replace	jogged	girlfriend
really	several	learned	perform
snapped	short	meaningful	pleasing
stands	slipped	opportunity	points
surgery	thorough	salary	ready
thousands	unhappy	spite	respond
today	wants	wonderful	terrify

161. GET YOUR HEAD INTO THIS ACTIVITY

Complete each of these 15 common expressions by inserting a different body part in each space. Select from the body parts listed here. Each body part is used only once.

1. strong _____ of the law

2. it's a _____ breaker

3. white-_____

4. gave her the cold _____

5. break-_____ speed

6. glad _____

7. _____ to the ground

8. _____-jerk reaction

9. has a glass _____

10. a _____ up on another

11. gave him _____ service

12. put his _____ in his _____

13. wore a poker _____

14. _____ grease

15. has no _____ for it

arm
back
ear
elbow
face
foot, mouth
hand
jaw
knee
knuckle
leg
lip
neck
shoulder
stomach

162. DRAW AND ENJOY

You deserve a break today! Even though you might not be the world's most famous artist, today you will draw—and enjoy the experience. Draw in each labeled box below. Or, if you prefer, use a separate sheet of plain paper for each. What will you learn about yourself?

The cover of your favorite book	**Your favorite literary character**
Your favorite possession	**Your favorite word**
Your favorite hobby	**Something you are good at**

163. YOUR BEDROOM

In the following essay, student-writer Kira Licata describes her bedroom. What are some of the writer's tools that she uses? Where does she begin the description? What particularly strong words are employed? After you and your classmates have discussed Kira's descriptive piece, write a description of your own bedroom on another sheet of paper. (Use the lines after this essay to jot down some of your ideas.) Your teacher will tell you how long your essay should be.

Van Gogh said, "The best way to know life is to love many things." Visiting this girl's room is a testament to that statement. As I climb the wooden stairs, I ascend towards a room of memories. A special place where a girl has grown up. A retreat from the outside world, her sanctuary. Crossing the threshold, my foot touches the cold wooden floor, aged with paint stains and scratches, clear signs of an active child. To the left there is an old antique bed. It creaks as I sit on the soft, cozy comforter. Enthroned atop the bed is a dirty white bear with scars on its nose; battle wounds from years of hugs. Looking down over the headboard is a framed poster of a female athlete famous in the world of soccer. She is probably the most prominent female role model in today's modern world. She represents opportunity and equality for women. As I focus on the adjacent wall, there appears to be a shrine to athleticism. Three photo plaques of victorious players portray the joys of winning state soccer championships. Other plaques recognize the hard work, leadership, and skill put into sports such as soccer, lacrosse, track, and basketball. All mark memories of seasons filled with success, disappointment, and the strong bonds of friendship.

There is another side to the girl portrayed on another wall. A poster of a circus scene by Seurat is framed and hanging above a desk. It is a souvenir from a nine-year-old-girl's trip to the Met. The wonders of pointillism so intricate were truly amazing to her. The desk is one of an avid worker. Piles of materials are neatly put to each corner. There's an alarm clock that has guided her through days, weeks, and years. The desk drawers are filled with various tools: pens, pencils, highlighters, and staplers for the schoolgirl side; markers, crayons, charcoal, and glue for the artist. One drawer is set aside for memories. It is filled with old playbills of various Broadway shows, letters from old friends, and pictures from over the years. There is also a small diary filled with collected quotations. Inspirational quotes, experiential quotes, movie quotes, and emotional quotes, each to fit a different mood that one might experience. Moving on to the right, my eyes move over a small bulletin board plastered with tickets from concerts and sporting events. There are pictures of best friends smiling, and flowers from the prom and one from an unforgettable day hung upside down. Under the windowsill is a yellow couch. It holds memories of childhood sleepovers. Those were nights that seemed to last forever, filled with whispers and secrets. A scent of burning wax drifts over from the corner, where a table holds a

163. YOUR BEDROOM (continued)

blue lava lamp and a small collection of candles. Each candle bears a story. The lava lamp was a present from her father on her 13ᵗʰ birthday, perhaps a gift that took him back to his own memories of that age. Jewelry of silver, gold, and beads cover the table. Some of her favorites are those she made herself. Drifting over towards the next panel, my eyes catch a large antique armoire. Inside there is a stereo surrounded by compact discs and tapes. The tapes date back from the 1980s, favorites from childhood. The discs cover a variety of music from classical to heavy metal with jazz and pop in between. The bulk of the wooden mass is filled with the scent of fabric softener wafting from a collection of soft wool sweaters. The other side is filled with books ranging from childhood favorites to beloved novels. One whole shelf has now come to be filled with college prep books, preparation for the tests that may somewhat determine her future. The final wall displays a hidden talent. Personal artwork hangs proudly, a mix of blues, greens, and reds.

The last evidence of the girl reminds me that she is a teenager. A magnetic poetry calendar is covered with movie stars, each portraying her favorite features: tall, dark, and handsome. Exiting the room and descending on the wooden stairs, I leave with a full feeling for the girl who grew up there. Over the years she has taken bits of art, music, sports, and friendships, and integrated them all into her life. She is a collection of her experiences.

164. GRANNY AND ODLUM'S

Student-writer Nora McGeough has written a memorable story about an experience from her childhood. She uses beautiful imagery through her detailed diction and varied syntax. Additionally, Nora has given us a glimpse of the wonderful experience she shared with her grandmother.

Your goal is to write a story that has the same power as Nora's. Begin by listing three memorable experiences from your past. Then select one of these events and brainstorm the experience. What details do you remember? Use your five senses to recreate this moment vividly. List them. Now decide how you would like to start the story to capture the reader's attention. Why do you want to start it this way? Lastly, include a fitting ending to your story.

Your teacher will tell you how long your story should be. Write convincingly and memorably!

The tabletop was a mottled pink. Its color was like the markings on a moth, yet unlike any moth, this table had experienced every summer holiday for three generations. The white paint that enveloped the legs was chipped and peeled, revealing earlier years of faded whites. (I remember secretly peeling off the paint, loving the rubber, waxy feeling that is so unlike the paint made today.) But it was only when the dinner plates had been cleared, the table dusted with clouds of all-purpose flour that my eager excitement wafted through the Irish kitchen. She would bring out a paper bag that had on its cover an orange owl wisely staring from a pair of horn-rimmed glasses. It was a bag of Odlum's Brown Bread Mix. The words still bring a nostalgic smile to my face reminding me of my grandmother, Nora, and the hours in which she helped to knead away my pre-teen troubles. Her wrinkled hands would carefully shake the water over the scattered flour, creating a freckled look upon the stainless steel bowl. I would relate my anecdotes from the morning, telling of the calf that was born or the forts that I had built. She would silently knead the dough, breathing heavily from lungs that were not previously aware that cigarettes are detrimental. When the kneading was complete, she would twist off a small piece of dough. (This was the part that I loved best.) Handing me that dough, I would create flowers, hearts, the letter N; it varied from time to time. Her two loaves never varied—oval shaped and crossed on the top. When all of our creations were popped into the oven, she would tidy the kitchen and fix the fire. She taught me to light the fire—briquettes of turf first, then blocks of split wood, and finally full logs. She taught me to spin the wheel on the bottom of the stove to let in air and keep the fire lit. By the time the fire was kindled and the floor swept, the bread would have turned golden brown. Our baked creations would emerge, mine usually a little crisp, and hers perfect. I would pour a glass of milk, cream still floating on top from the morning's milking. She would take out my favorite loganberry jam, another of her original creations. I would eat the crust first and then, saving the best for last, roll the inside into a doughy ball and savor it. Cutting away at the ends of the bread, I never dreamed that our time together was also being cut away.

164. GRANNY AND ODLUM'S (continued)

As the years went on, I did not relish the idea of spending all summer on the farm. Forts no longer intrigued me. I had already seen dozens of calves being born and had milked hundreds of cows, yet I would never get sick of making bread. The "kneaded time" with my grandmother was getting more and more infrequent. During my last two summers on my grandparents' farm, I was lucky if we made bread twice. When my grandmother passed away, I did not cry. I knew that I would miss her and that my summers would never be the same. Her lessons though, no matter how small, will stay with me forever. In building the fire, she taught me patience. If it did not catch the first time, she told me to keep the wood in a tripod until it did. She encouraged perfection by telling me to take my various bread shapes out earlier so they would not burn. She showed me how to finish what I started by making sure that every crumb or dusting of flour was properly cleaned up. The most important, yet hardest lesson for me, was revealed through her death. The lesson is that opportunity is transient. She taught me to love learning and to take every opportunity to expand my mind. The lesson could be learning to milk cows, drive a tractor, solve a mathematical equation, row a crew boat, learn about a new culture, or even make bread. Some of these lessons might seem trivial to a teenager living in suburban New York, but I know that not everyone is given the opportunities that I have been given, and I want to make the most of each one.

All of these lessons had their genesis in the simple act of making bread. In the heat of New York summers, when my Irish skin turns a deep red, and I am trying to keep cool, ironically, I turn on the oven. The connection between my namesake and me is strongest when I make that Odlum's Brown Bread. My grandmother taught her lessons in a time and place much different from today's fast-paced, often stressful world. These were more than bread-making lessons. They were lessons in life. Now, years later, as I write a challenging essay, debate a controversial issue, or yes, even as I make brown bread using Odlum's Mix, I often think about the lessons my grandmother taught me, and silently thank her for instilling in me the ingredients to lead a happy, successful life.

165. START THE WORLD'S NEXT CIVILIZATION

Here are your seven chances to truly make a difference. Pretend you have the opportunity to begin a new and improved civilization. Select seven literary characters who would be the first seven citizens of this new civilization. Remember, you have to continue the civilization so you must select members of both sexes. We need people who can build, people who can medically treat others, people who can teach others, and much more. Yet, *you* have the most important role because you get to select the seven who will start it all.

On the lines below, select the seven characters. Tell why you have chosen each person and what that person's role will be in this new civilization. (Use another sheet of paper if you need more space for your answers.) When you have finished, discuss your choices with your classmates.

Character #1: _____

_____

Character #2: _____

_____

Character #3: _____

_____

Character #4: _____

_____

Character #5: _____

_____

Character #6: _____

_____

Character #7: _____

_____

166. EXACTLY WHO ARE YOU?

Here are a few questions that will help you and others learn more about yourself. Answer the following questions and share the answers—if you choose to. Either way, you will find out a bit more about yourself in the process.

1. A song that makes me happy is _____.

It makes me happy because _____

_____.

2. A television program that makes me laugh is _____

because _____

_____.

3. A book that has made me think about how people treat each other is _____

_____. This is because _____

_____

_____.

4. I would like to be like the literary character _____

because _____

_____

_____.

5. A relative I look up to is _____

because _____

_____

_____.

6. Today, the people of the world need to _____

_____.

166. EXACTLY WHO ARE YOU? (continued)

7. The world's best sport is _____

because _____

_____.

8. The animal I most resemble is the _____

because _____

_____.

9. The musical instrument I most resemble is the _____

because _____

_____.

10. My favorite children's story character is _____

because _____

_____,

11. Three very important events in my life include (A) _____

_____, (B) _____,

and (C) _____.

12. In twenty years I will be working as a(n) _____.

I will enjoy this work because _____

_____.

13. Three adjectives that describe me are _____,

_____, and _____.

14. Four adjectives that describe one of my best friends are _____,

_____, _____, and _____.

15. A motto I try to follow is _____

because _____.

167. HOW MUCH ARE YOU LIKE YOUR FRIENDS AND CLASSMATES?

Through today's brainstorming, you can see to what extent you and your friends think alike. In the space provided, list your thoughts regarding the following questions. Just write down whatever comes into your head during the one minute given to you. When the minute is over, compare your answers with those of your classmates. In this way, you can see who thinks the same way you do! Enjoy!

1. What are some words that describe an effective leader?

2. What are some events or things we celebrate?

3. What are some items found in a baby's room?

4. What inventions have had the biggest influence on your life?

5. What are some problems many teens face?

6. What words describe your best friend(s)?

7. Name some items found in most basements.

8. List things associated with scary movies.

9. List some milestones in a person's life.

10. List some changes that would improve today's world.

168. IF I WERE . . .

Sit back. Relax. Think. Let your mind do all the work. You will enjoy this assignment because *you* are the focus of *every* question. Write your answers on the lines provided.

1. If I were a season, I would be _____

because _____

_____.

2. If I were a planet, I would be _____

because _____

_____.

3. If I were a weather condition (for example, sunshine, snow, rain, hail), I would be _____

_____ because _____

_____.

4. If I were a color, I would be the color _____

because _____

_____.

5. If I were a magazine, I would be _____

because _____

_____.

6. If I were a sea creature, I would be a(n) _____

because _____

_____.

7. If I were a car, I would be a(n) _____

because _____

_____.

168. IF I WERE . . . (continued)

8. If I were a type of road (such as dirt road, highway, expressway, boulevard, lane), I would

be a(n) _____

because _____

_____.

9. If I were a type of building (for example, house of worship, school, barn, mall, castle), I

would be a(n) _____

because _____

_____.

10. If I were a tool or utensil (for example, hammer, saw, wrench, spoon, fork), I would be

a(n) _____

because _____

_____.

11. If I were a movie, I would be _____

because _____.

12. If I were a body of water (such as lake, ocean, stream, canal), I would be a(n) _____

_____ because _____

_____.

13. If I were a type of footwear, I would be a(n) _____

because _____.

14. If I were a dessert, I would be a(n) _____

because _____

_____.

15. If I were a foreign country, I would be _____

because _____.

169. THINKING LITERARILY

Authors make us think. The conflicts, characters, and settings they create are food for thought. If done correctly, these writers inspire us to consider our own existences. How does your world compare to that of some of your favorite literary characters? How are their surroundings similar to or different from yours? Here is the opportunity to consider your world and the literary world at the same time. Answer these questions, and then discuss your thoughts with your classmates.

1. (A) Name a literary character who shares at least three positive characteristics with you.

_____

   (B) What are the three characteristics? _____

_____

_____

   (C) Give an illustrative example of how that character exhibits each characteristic.

1st characteristic: _____

_____

2nd characteristic: _____

_____

3rd characteristic: _____

_____

2. (A) Cite a literary work that features a character who displays behaviors you find

intolerable. _____

   (B) What is the behavior? _____

_____

   (C) What factors contribute to this behavior? _____

_____

_____

169. THINKING LITERARILY (continued)

3. (A) Cite a literary work whose setting you enjoy. _____

_____

(B) Why do you like this setting? _____

_____

(C) How would you improve this setting? _____

_____

4. (A) Cite a work that displays an admirable relationship between two people. _____

_____

(B) What makes this relationship admirable? _____

_____

_____

(C) How could this relationship be improved? _____

_____

_____

5. (A) Which book author do you think you would like to meet? _____

_____

(B) Why? _____

_____

(C) What are several questions you would ask him or her? _____

_____

_____

_____

_____

170. WHAT WILL THE FUTURE BRING?

Many different occupations are listed below. Place a check next to the five you would most like to do when you become an adult. Next to each of those five, write three traits that are necessary in order to do well in that position. Finally, on a separate sheet of paper, write down ten things that this list has taught you about yourself. Enjoy learning about yourself!

☐ accountant: _____

☐ airline pilot: _____

☐ artist: _____

☐ author: _____

☐ chief executive officer: _____

☐ construction worker: _____

☐ detective: _____

☐ doctor: _____

☐ lawyer: _____

☐ librarian: _____

☐ model: _____

☐ newspaper reporter: _____

☐ office manager: _____

☐ photographer: _____

☐ playwright: _____

☐ police officer: _____

☐ professional athlete: _____

☐ radio personality: _____

☐ religious leader: _____

☐ salesperson: _____

☐ stockbroker: _____

☐ teacher: _____

☐ television personality: _____

_____ (your choice): _____

_____ (your choice): _____

_____ (your choice): _____

171. HOW GOOD CAN ONE BE?

Have you ever imagined what the perfect literary character would be like? What traits would that person have? Would he or she be kind, intelligent, wealthy, or healthy? What makes this character so special?

Next to each trait below, write the name of a literary character you have encountered. Then, on the other side of this sheet, select an instance in which the character exhibited that trait. Select a different character for each trait. You can select any character who appears in a novel, play, short story, poem, or nursery rhyme. When you have finished writing a character for each trait, you will have constructed the perfect literary character! Discuss your answers with your classmates.

1. ABILITY TO OVERCOME DIFFICULTIES: _____

2. APPEARANCE: _____

3. ATHLETIC ABILITY: _____

4. DECISION-MAKING: _____

5. RESOLVING A FAMILY PROBLEM: _____

6. FRIENDLINESS: _____

7. HEALTH: _____

8. INTELLIGENCE: _____

9. KINDNESS: _____

10. MORALS: _____

11. PERSEVERANCE: _____

12. SENSE OF HUMOR: _____

13. WORK HABITS: _____

172. WHAT WOULD THEY DO?

Have you ever imagined that some literary characters came to life? How would they react in real-life situations? Would you be proud of their actions or would you wish they had acted differently?

First, list three memorable literary characters. Then, on the lines following the three life situations, tell how you think each character would act in that situation. Be ready to support your answers, based on the actions he or she displayed in the literary work, in a class discussion.

Literary character #1: _____

Literary character #2: _____

Literary character #3: _____

> **Situation A:** A wallet containing several hundred dollars is on the floor near the exit doors of the local mall. Several pieces of identification, including a driver's license, clearly indicate the wallet's owner. No one else sees the literary character pick up the wallet. What would he or she do?

Literary character #1: _____

_____

Literary character #2: _____

_____

Literary character #3: _____

_____

172. WHAT WOULD THEY DO? (continued)

Situation B: You and your best friend had a verbal argument last week. Now, eight days later, you and your friend have still not spoken to each other. What would each character probably do (or not do) in this situation?

Literary character #1: _____

_____

Literary character #2: _____

_____

Literary character #3: _____

_____

Situation C: Students in your school want to sponsor a fund drive to help poor people in a neighboring community. Some town residents support the idea, while others are against it. A town meeting is held, and each of your literary characters speaks at this meeting. What would each say?

Literary character #1: _____

_____

Literary character #2: _____

_____

Literary character #3: _____

_____

173. TRY THESE TEN TOUGH TONGUE TWISTERS TODAY

It's time to test your tongue-twisting talent today. With a classmate or two, try to clearly say each tongue twister. Then, using a dictionary if you need to, revise these ten tongue twisters so they sound nothing like the original, but they still have the same meaning. When a proper name is used, retain it in the revision. Write the revised editions on the appropriate lines. Have fun!

1. Nice, neat Neal knelt near Nellie for nearly ninety-nine minutes. _____

_____

2. The sixth sick sheik's sixth sheep's sick. _____

_____

3. Friendly, funny Fred found fifty-five fearless female firefighters. _____

_____

4. Toy boat. Toy boat. Toy boat. _____

_____

5. Barbara Bobrow's brother borrowed Bill Bentley's big bicycle. _____

_____

6. Shy Suzy sat on a sandy, shellacked shell Saturday. _____

_____

7. Old oily oilmen ought to avoid autos, Ollie. _____

_____

8. Pathetic Peter probably pilfered plenty of pickled peppers. _____

_____

9. Slowly, steadily, and surely, Sherry said she saw the big black bear. _____

_____

10. Go grapple Greg's gorilla, Gary. _____

_____

174. JUST DROPPING IN

Travel into worlds you never thought you would be able to before today! All you have to do is think and then write your thoughts here. Right, you will not be there in person, but you will be there in spirit, and that is good enough! Just dropping in is fine for now! Share your thoughts with your classmates.

1. I would like to be placed in the setting of the television program _____

_____ because _____

_____.

2. I would like to be placed in the setting of the play _____

_____ because _____

_____

_____.

3. I would like to be placed in the setting of the novel _____

_____ because _____

_____.

4. I would like to be in the rock group _____

because _____

_____.

5. I would like to be on the professional sports team _____

because _____

_____.

174. JUST DROPPING IN (continued)

6. I would like to be placed in the setting of the movie _____

_____ because _____

_____

_____.

7. I would like to be placed in the fictional school setting of _____

_____ because _____

_____

_____.

8. I would like to be living in the historical period of _____

_____ because _____

_____

_____.

9. I would like to have been at the historic sports moment _____

_____ because _____

_____

_____.

10. I would like to have the job of _____

for a week because _____

_____

_____.

175. DISCUSSING AND DECIDING

Here are ten topics that should spark some discussion. For each topic, list your three answers. Then, within your group, discuss your answers. Finally, see if your group can come to some agreement on these topics. Have fun!

1. Three of the world's most serious problems:_____

_____

2. Three books that every student my age should read: _____

_____

3. Three words that have a funny sound to them: _____

_____

4. Three songs that have important things to say: _____

_____

5. Three historical figures who changed the world: _____

_____

6. Three ways my generation is different from my parents' generation: _____

_____

7. Three ways the world has changed for the better in the last 25 years:_____

_____

8. Three major concerns of most teens: _____

_____

9. Three countries I would like to visit: _____

_____

10. Three magazines that many teens like to read: _____

_____

176. EACH THREE WILL HELP YOU TO SEE
(MORE ABOUT YOURSELF)

Write three answers within each of the following ten groups. After completing the groups, answer these questions on a separate sheet of paper: **(1)** What four things have you learned about yourself from your answers? **(2)** What two things have you learned about yourself that you feel are typical for a person your age? **(3)** What one thing have you learned about yourself that you feel is a bit different for someone your age? **(4)** What category do you wish had appeared on this page? You might want to share your answers with your classmates.

1. Your three favorite books: _____

_____

2. Your three favorite movies: _____

_____

3. Your three favorite words (no vulgar words): _____

_____

4. Your three favorite activities: _____

_____

5. Your three role models: _____

_____

6. Your three favorite television shows: _____

_____

7. Your three favorite possessions: _____

_____

8. Your three favorite holidays: _____

_____

9. Three actions you find totally unacceptable: _____

_____

10. Your three favorite fictional characters: _____

_____

177. BUILD THE PERFECT PERSON

Okay, it's time to compose your perfect person. How? Simple. Next to each physical feature and personal characteristic below, write the name of the literary character you feel best exemplifies that feature or characteristic. You can use the same character any number of times. You may even choose an animal from a literary work! If, after a while, you are not sure of an answer, leave it blank. Discuss your answers with your classmates.

1. face: _____

2. build: _____

3. health: _____

4. willpower: _____

5. loyalty: _____

6. honesty: _____

7. intelligence: _____

8. friendliness: _____

9. work ethic: _____

10. open-mindedness: _____

11. tolerance: _____

12. trust: _____

13. happiness: _____

14. humility: _____

15. charity: _____

16. humor: _____

17. kindness: _____

18. decision-making ability: _____

19. financial stability: _____

20. temperament: _____

178. THINKING AND WRITING

How would your life change if you had only two weeks off from school each year? Could you make it for a month without your radio, television, computer, and CD player? Do some thinking and writing about these and the eight other scenarios. On the lines provided (or on another sheet of paper), show the changes that would take place in your life if each of these occurred. Talk over your answers with your classmates.

How would your life be different if . . .

1. . . . the school day were only 3 hours long? _____

_____

_____

2. . . . each day were 48 hours long? _____

_____

_____

3. . . . soccer was played with 4 instead of 11 players on a team? _____

_____

_____

4. . . . colors were eliminated? _____

_____

_____

5. . . . you could not use your radio, television, computer, or CD player for a month? _____

_____

_____

178. THINKING AND WRITING (continued)

6. . . . you celebrated your 65th birthday tomorrow? _____

_____

_____

7. . . . your radio, instead of picking up radio stations, picked up conversations in

neighboring apartments or houses instead? _____

_____

_____

8. . . . everyone in your English class started to speak a language you did not understand?

_____

_____

9. . . . you only had two weeks off from school each year? _____

_____

_____

10. . . . you had a third eye located on the tip of your right hand's index finger?

_____

_____

179. THE DESCRIPTIVE YOU

Here is your chance to take a good look at your positive qualities. For each letter A–Z, write an adjective that begins with that particular letter and that accurately describes you. If you can fill in more than one word for any of the letters, do so. After all, this is your chance to brag about yourself!

A. _____   N. _____

B. _____   O. _____

C. _____   P. _____

D. _____   Q. _____

E. _____   R. _____

F. _____   S. _____

G. _____   T. _____

H. _____   U. _____

I. _____   V. _____

J. _____   W. _____

K. _____   X. _____

L. _____   Y. _____

M. _____   Z. _____

180. THE PERFECT DAY

Have you ever dreamed of a day in which you could do anything you wanted? On that day, you could go where you wanted and do what you wanted. Well, today you will construct your own perfect day. Your only restriction is time. You must complete your day in 24 hours. Money is no object!

Ten locations have been given to you. You can add any five of your own to the list. On a separate sheet of paper, write the itinerary (list of activities along with the time spent on each activity) for your day (and perhaps night). Then, in the space below, write five things you have learned about yourself based on the choices you made on how you would spend the day. Share your answers with your classmates.

AIRPORT	MOVIES
AMUSEMENT PARK	PARK
DOCK	RESTAURANT
LIBRARY	SCHOOL
MALL	SPORTS ARENA

(YOUR CHOICE) _____

(YOUR CHOICE) _____

(YOUR CHOICE) _____

(YOUR CHOICE) _____

(YOUR CHOICE) _____

Five things I've learned about myself:

_____

_____

_____

_____

_____

181. WOULD YOU RATHER . . . ?

Here are 15 situations in which you are asked to make a decision. Circle your choice. Then, on a separate sheet of paper, give three reasons for your preference. Your teacher will tell you whether the reasons should be written in complete sentences. After that, discuss your reasons with the students in your group. Be open to the opinions and feelings of your classmates.

Would you rather . . .

1. write a hit song **OR** invent something useful for people?

2. be very popular **OR** be very smart?

3. have health **OR** wealth?

4. live on a sparsely populated island **OR** live in a crowded, bustling city?

5. be your school's principal **OR** the school's most respected teacher?

6. be a decorated war hero **OR** a decorated police officer?

7. be a politician **OR** an architect?

8. be your country's president **OR** the owner of a major sports team?

9. be the president of your class **OR** the student voted "Best Looking"?

10. set a world's record in a sport **OR** save a young child from drowning?

11. be loyal **OR** be honest?

12. spend a month in the mountains **OR** spend that time in a home overlooking the ocean?

13. visit a senior citizens' home to read to the residents **OR** do the same at a hospital for terminally-ill children?

14. own a small business in your hometown **OR** be the police chief in that town?

15. write a best-selling novel **OR** write a number-one song?

ANSWER KEY

Section One: This Is Not Your Grandma's Grammar

1. SCAN, SORT, AND EARN

Here are some of the words found in the puzzle. There will be additional ones.

arch	bleat	deal	heart	scan	sort
balk	can't	dealt	heat	scare	sorted
bear	care	diet	hook	scared	table
bide	chalk	earn	hoot	shed	tabled
bite	cheat	heal	learn	shook	talk
blare	crab	hear	rook	shoot	tide
					tier

2. LINKING IT UP

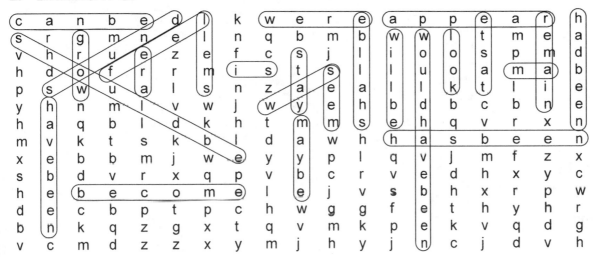

3. LISTEN TO YOURSELF

Answers will vary. The following answers are suggestions:

One-syllable nouns are *man, girl, boy,* and *toy*.
One-syllable verbs are *hit, run, lift,* and *use*.
One-syllable adjectives are *cute, tall, smart,* and *right*.

Two-syllable nouns are *woman, machine, window,* and *loser*.
Two-syllable verbs are *wonder, swindle, survive,* and *function*.
Two-syllable adjectives are *taller, correct, precise,* and *faithful*.

Three-syllable nouns are *beginning, resources, saxophone,* and *outfielder*.
Three-syllable verbs are *remember, stimulate, vegetate,* and *dominate*.
Three-syllable adjectives are *forgetful, meaningful, courteous,* and *malnourished*.

Four-syllable nouns are *automobile, machinery, ineptitude,* and *self-assurance*.
Four-syllable verbs are *indoctrinate, procrastinate, invigorate,* and *commiserate*.
Four-syllable adjectives are *indecisive, insufficient, notorious,* and *resistible*.

4. ADJECTIVE HUNT

The following 25 adjectives should be circled:

apprehensive	definitive	large	past	soluble
bigger	guiding	last	pronounced	strong
biographical	impressive	lost	reliable	supplementary
conclusive	independent	masterful	similar	sweltering
controversial	interesting	orderly	soft	voluntary

5. MOVE IT ON!

Answers will vary.

6. VERBS AND PRONOUNS GALORE!

These 10 verbs should be circled:

are	maltreat
begin	melt
fix	seize
had	stand
kick	varying

These 10 pronouns should be boxed:

each	nobody
he	none
I	ourselves
mine	several
myself	them

7. AND THE OTHERS?

1. noun
2. adverb
3. verb, adjective, adverb
4. adjective, noun, adverb, interjection
5. verb, adjective
6. noun
7. noun
8. noun
9. adjective, verb
10. noun, adjective
11. verb
12. noun, adjective
13. verb, adjective, adverb
14. noun, verb
15. noun, verb

8. PROBING FOR PRONOUNS

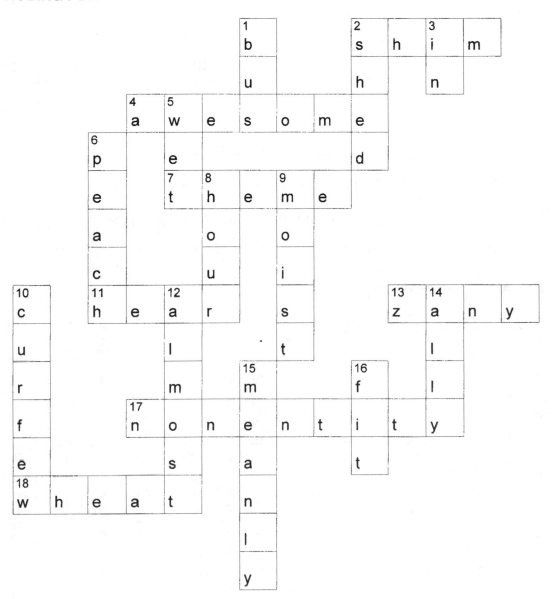

The pronouns are:

Across: 2. him; 4. we; 7. them; 11. he; 13. any; 17. it; 18. he

Down: 1. us; 2. he; 3. I; 5. we; 6. each; 8. our; 9. I; 10. few; 12. most; 14. all; 15. me; 16. it

9. PLENTY OF PREPOSITIONS

1. AGAINST
2. OVER
3. BELOW
4. DOWN
5. BEFORE

6. INTO
7. PAST
8. ABOVE
9. OF
10. ABOUT

11. UNDER
12. BEHIND
13. AT
14. DURING
15. FROM

16. WITH
17. AFTER
18. FOR
19. THROUGHOUT
20. ACROSS

Letter Substitution Code
A B C D E F G H I L M N O P R S T U V W
G L N I S D C T U M B W H V A R O F E P

10. IT'S ALL IN THE FAMILY

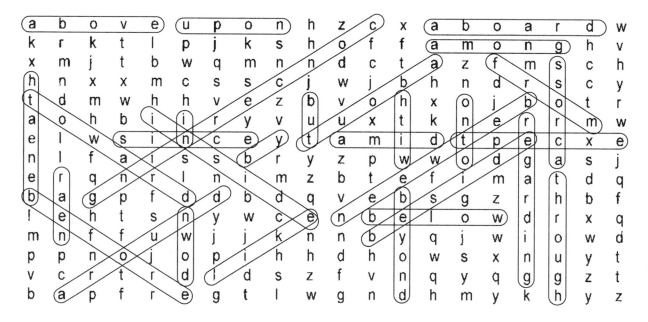

11. SEEING ALLITERATIVELY

Answers will vary. These are suggestions:

agile antelopes
brown buttons
colorful cartoons
dark drapes
eager egrets
friendly fellows
gorgeous guests
handsome hosts
interesting irons

jovial jumpers
knobby knees
little lamps
monstrous mountains
new nails
open offices
pretty pictures
quick quails
rusty rails

shallow streams
thin thistles
unmasked umpires
violent vipers
wild walruses
xanthous xylophones
yellow yaks
zany zebras

12. HOW VERSATILE ARE THESE WORDS?
1. (ON) preposition, (EW) adverb, (AT) adjective, (CH) verb, (ES) noun
2. (CE) adjective
3. (LL) verb
4. (S,) adjective
5. (AN) adjective, (DT) noun, (HE) verb
6. (OT) adjective
7. (HE) adjective, (RS) verb, (EL) noun
8. (LS) verb, (WA) noun
9. (TC) noun, (HE) verb
10. (S!) adjective

Answer to riddle: ONE WATCHES CELLS, AND THE OTHER SELLS WATCHES!

13. GRAMMAR TERMS ON PARADE
Selection One:
Adjective phrase: for Bettsbridge
Verb phrase: had once more eased
Adverb: Only
Adverb phrase: on him
Consecutive adverbs: so clearly

Selection Two:
Adverb phrase: in the days
Adverb: just
Conjunction: and
Pronoun/adjective: this
Adjective: nappy
Clause: when everyone was old or stupid or young and foolish

14. PARTS-OF-SPEECH MAGIC SQUARE

A=13	B=16	C=24	D=2	E=10
F=22	G=5	H=8	I=11	J=19
K=6	L=14	M=17	N=25	O=3
P=20	Q=23	R=1	S=9	T=12
U=4	V=7	W=15	X=18	Y=21

Columns, rows, and diagonals add up to 65.

15. HIDDEN COUNTRIES

1. France—verb
2. Germany—noun, adjective
3. Poland—noun, verb
4. Argentina—noun, adjective
5. Cameroon—verb
6. Spain—noun, verb
7. Italy—pronoun
8. Turkey—noun, verb, adjective
9. Finland—noun
10. Hungary—verb
11. Pakistan—noun, verb
12. Singapore—noun, verb
13. Scotland—noun
14. Andorra—conjunction
15. Chad—verb
16. Denmark—noun
17. Ireland—noun
18. Jordan—conjunction
19. Nicaragua—noun
20. Paraguay—noun, verb, adjective

16. VERBALLY SPEAKING

1. I
2. I
3. G
4. P
5. P
6. G
7. P
8. G
9. P
10. I
11. G
12. G
13. I
14. I
15. P

G = 3 + 6 + 8 + 11 + 12 = 40
P = 4 + 5 + 7 + 9 + 15 = 40
I = 1 + 2 + 10 + 13 + 14 = 40

17. 25 WITH 4 HAVE 2

A=1	B=10	C=19	D=23	E=12
F=18	G=22	H=11	I=5	J=9
K=15	L=4	M=8	N=17	O=21
P=7	Q=16	R=25	S=14	T=3
U=24	V=13	W=2	X=6	Y=20

Columns, rows, and diagonals add up to 65.

18. FIRST NAMES ONLY

1. P	5. M	12. E	17. C
2. E	6. A	13. L	18. H
3. L	7. D	14. V	19. E
4. E	8. O	15. I	20. R
	9. N	16. S	
	10. N		
	11. A		

The four famous first names are PELE (the soccer player), and MADONNA, ELVIS, and CHER (all singer-entertainers).

19. SPELLING THE PLURALS

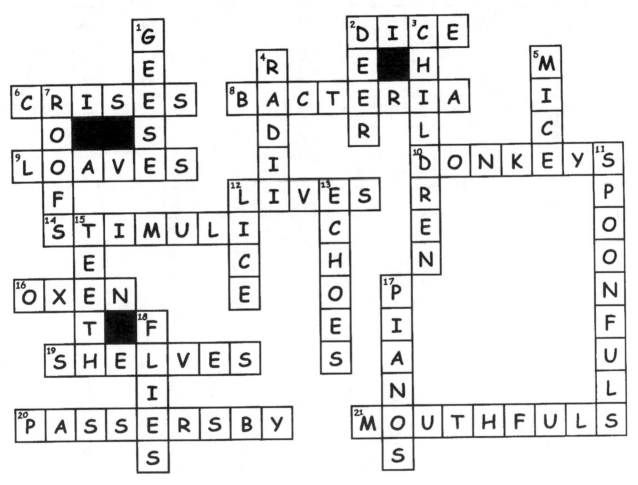

20. MISSPELLINGS

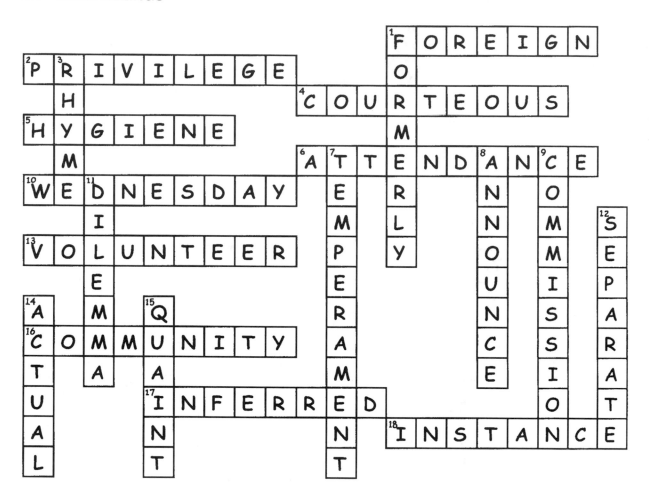

21. FIX UP THESE 20 MISSPELLINGS

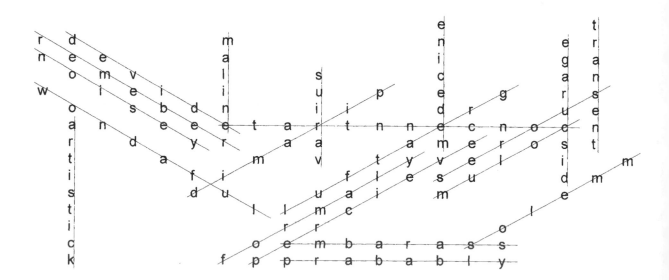

artistic	embarrass	noisy	serious
column	formally	perceive	solemn
concentrate	grateful	pyramid	transient
divide	malign	probably	various
discourage	medicine	remember	wonderful

22. GRAMMAR AND MECHANICS
1. C
2. B
3. C
4. C
5. B
6. A
7. B
8. B
9. B
10. C

23. THREE ON A MATCH
1. The EMT lifted the patient into the van.
2. The umpire ejected the player from the game.
3. The seagull picked the food from the garbage.
4. The surfer rode the waves toward the shore.
5. The professor demonstrated the problem on the chalkboard.
6. The vendor gave the change to the customer.
7. The surgeon performed the surgery in the OR.
8. The magician pulled the rabbit out of the hat.
9. The florist arranged the flowers for the wedding.
10. The lawyer questioned the witness during the trial.

The 4 trees: BIRCH, CEDAR, CYPRESS, FIR

24. STRUCTURING SENTENCES
Sentences will vary. Here are suggestions:

1. Both the boys and the girls entered the large cafeteria.
2. I wanted to hire the candidate who had the higher score.
3. The jury met briefly on Friday afternoon.
4. Laurie lost Lucy's locket.
5. She and he studied the material and quizzed each other last Wednesday night.
6. Brenda and she saw the models wearing the stylish red dresses last fall.
7. Did they compete in that marathon?
8. They made and then delivered the presents to their relatives.
9. Chris and Jim traveled far in their new automobile.
10. In the morning, clean your room.
11. The boy in the fourth row wanted to ask a question.
12. Does that girl sitting by herself want to join us here?
13. Let's go to the mall now.
14. Sitting for those three hours was not easy for the three young boys.
15. When will everyone see the results of the test?

25. WHERE DID THE VOWELS GO?
1. We can go to the store now.
2. Some people love to sing and dance.
3. Please turn off the radio.
4. Did you finish your homework assignments?
5. They have never purchased older cars.
6. Flies and bees are annoying to picnickers.
7. The weather has not been that warm this week.
8. Make the intelligent decision soon.

26. SENTENCES—LETTER BY LETTER
Sentences will vary. These are suggestions:

1. All boys obey very eagerly.
2. Small tigers are really terrific.
3. Each volunteer earned respect yesterday.
4. Seldom will everybody enjoy pasta.
5. Ask Ursula to honor our request.
6. Today each actor called home.
7. Happy elves loved praising Santa.
8. Speaking eloquently, Laura delivered our message.
9. Nearly everybody watched Sue preview and perform each role.
10. Obviously, very elegant, rich people own wonderfully expensive rings.

27. BY THE LETTERS
Sentences will vary. These are suggestions:

1. Tomorrow is another day.
2. You must remember these answers.
3. Seeing the program inspired Rita and her.
4. Several people are in the house now.
5. Will the champion be ready?
6. Grab the raft, Steve.
7. Isaac has to get to class now.
8. How many concerts have you gone to this year?
9. None of the workers heard the alarm.
10. Which wrestler will be the county champion?
11. Our car will be in the repair shop for the next few days.
12. The mall was very crowded during the holidays.
13. Send it to me immediately.
14. He will coach both teams this winter.
15. The story read by Adam was interesting.

28. SENTENCES, FRAGMENTS, AND RUN-ONS
The sentences are numbers 2, 5, 8, 13, 14, and 15. They spell out YOU LOOK GREAT.
The fragments are numbers 1, 4, 6, 9, 10, and 12. They spell out THE BABY CRIED.
The run-ons are numbers 3, 7, and 11. They spell out I MAY GO.

29. SENTENCE STUFF

The completed crossword puzzle contains the following answers:

Across
3. COMPOUND
9. RUN ON
10. SIMPLE
11. IMPERATIVE
12. COMMA
13. EXCLAMATORY

Down
1. QUESTION MARK
2. DECLARATIVE
4. PERIOD
5. PREDICATE
6. SUBJECT
7. FRAGMENT
8. INTERROGATIVE
3. CONDITIONAL
12. COMPLEX

Section Two: Playing With Words

30. MAKING THE CONNECTION

These words can be made in the word grid. There are probably others as well.

ache	cheat	hate	shut	teach
cart	crack	heat	skat	that
char	crate	race	skate	these
chart	cute	seat	tack	trace
chat	hack	shake	taut	tuck

31. JUST SAY NO!

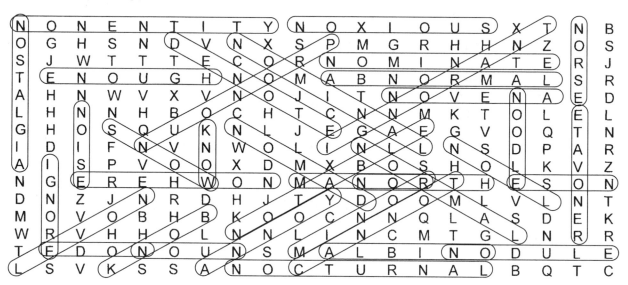

32. ONE WANTS TO HELP YOU!

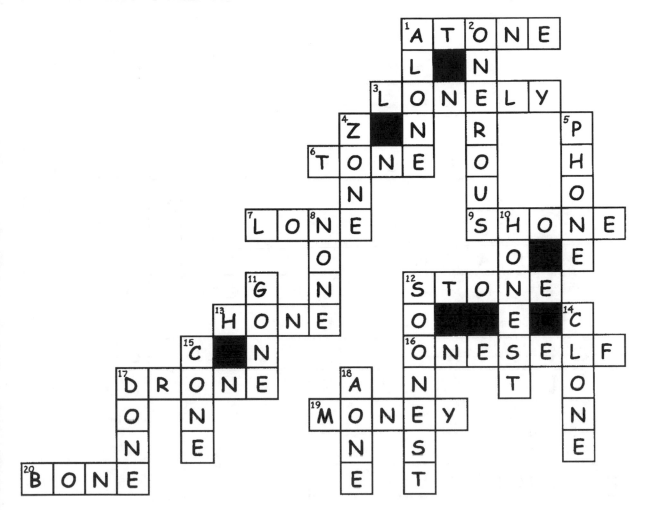

33. MIND YOUR P'S AND Q'S

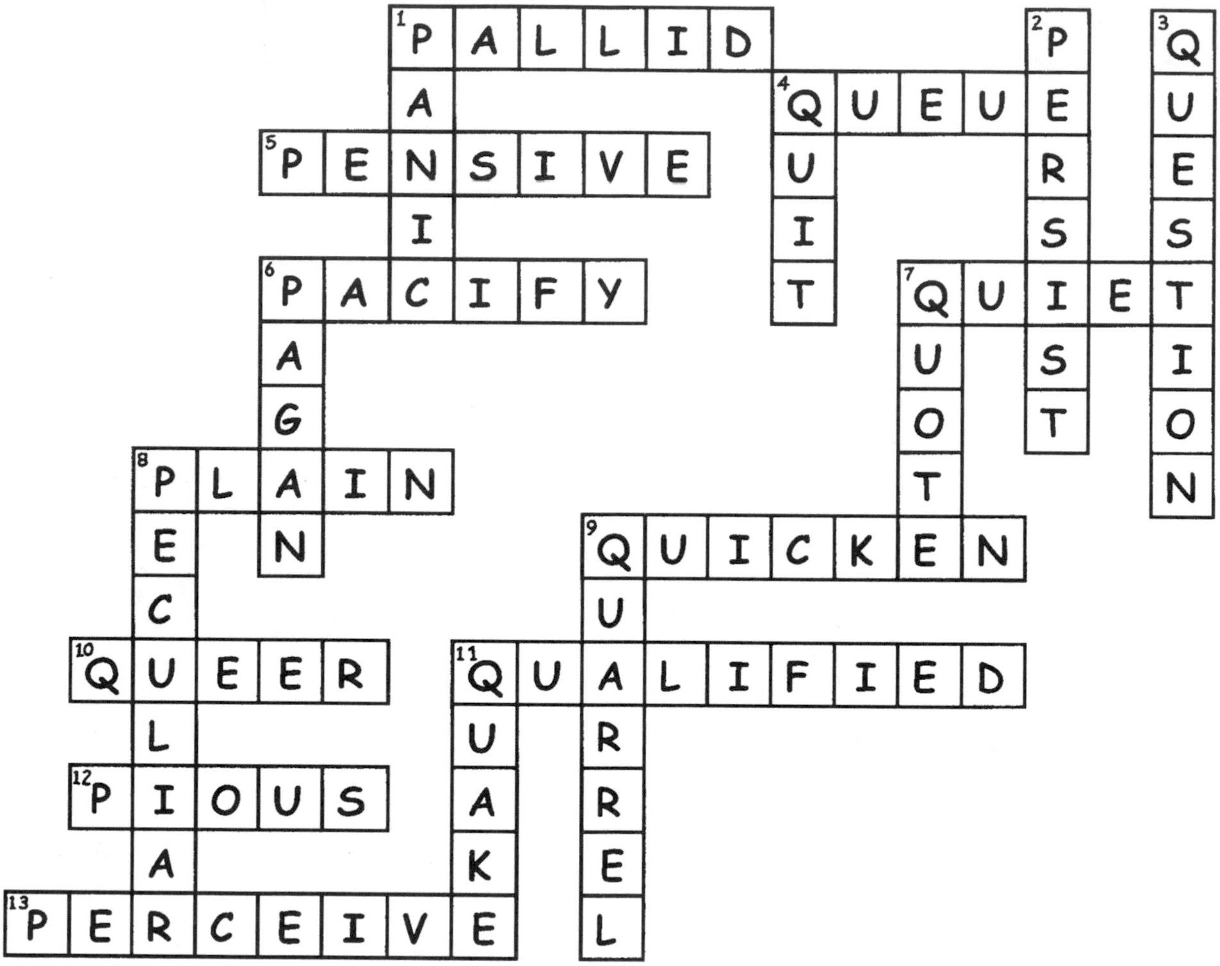
1 PALLID
2 PERSIST
3 QUESTION
4 QUEUE
5 PENSIVE
6 PACIFY
7 QUIET
8 PLAIN
9 QUICKEN
10 QUEER
11 QUALIFIED
12 PIOUS
13 PERCEIVE
PANIC
QUIT
PAGAN
QUOTE
PECULIAR
QUARREL
QUAKE

34. FIND THE RIGHT SPOT!

1. billet (bet + ill)
2. frisked (fed + risk)
3. important (import + tan)
4. presently (ply + resent)
5. pleasure (pure + leas)
6. shallow (show + all)
7. stoplight (slight + top)
8. swallow (sow + wall)
9. straying (sting + ray)
10. wheeling (wing + heel)

35. THE UNNEEDED LETTERS ARE NEEDED

Group One: What a Waste!
1. satire
2. saucy
3. toxic
4. giggle
5. reject

The new word: DROSS

Group Two: A Real Low Point!
1. humble
2. chasm
3. exalt
4. tripod
5. vain

The new word: NADIR

Group Three: Break Out!
1. vogue
2. toupee
3. atlas
4. evict
5. abyss

The new word: ERUPT

36. THREE'S COMPANY

allotment	daughters	investors	political
bothering	elegantly	mortgages	prejudice
calculate	encourage	objective	strategic
character	financial	obstacles	thousands
concerned	gemstones	otherwise	universal

37. THREE'S A CHARM

1. abstract
2. anatomy
3. comprehend
4. convenient
5. decorate
6. efficiency
7. exquisite
8. impulsive
9. manifest
10. obvious
11. optional
12. property
13. provision
14. psychologist
15. reliable

38. HOW DO 26 LETTERS DISAPPEAR SO EASILY?

1. amazing
2. annoy
3. arrest
4. attest
5. aquamarine
6. bayou
7. bazaar
8. benign
9. elegant
10. essence
11. giraffe
12. hijack
13. hurrah
14. hymn
15. maximum
16. mellow
17. neighbor
18. wonderful
19. picnicking
20. prowl
21. radii
22. reception
23. riddance
24. savvy
25. vaccine
26. vacuum

39. UNSCRAMBLING THE SCRAMBLED

Jumble #1	Jumble #2	Jumble #3	Jumble #4
1. LYRES	1. MIRED	1. VALET	1. LIVID
2. GRIPE	2. IDIOT	2. TREND	2. SEEKS
3. NOTED	3. CROON	3. QUILT	3. BRISK
4. BOOST	4. TEARY	4. TRESS	4. TOKEN
Answer:	*Answer:*	*Answer:*	*Answer:*
STOOL PIGEON	DIRTY ROOM	QUARTERS	IKE'S BIKES

40. A STATELY ACTIVITY

1. DETAIL
2. MANHANDLE
3. HIMSELF
4. GALLANT
5. ARGUMENT
6. SCALE
7. FLOOR
8. SECOND
9. WINNER
10. VARIETY
11. INDUCTION
12. MISDIRECT
13. WARMTH
14. MONKS
15. CARRIAGE

41. JUMPING FROM JUMBLE TO JUMBLE

Jumble #1	Jumble #2	Jumble #3	Jumble #4
1. SLICE	1. LEECH	1. ANSWER	1. WHALE
2. TAUNT	2. METAL	2. FEISTY	2. ELEGY
3. EERIE	3. SCOUR	3. WOUND	3. ABYSS
4. SLANT	4. WANTS	4. BRINE	4. LEGAL
Answer:	*Answer:*	*Answer:*	*Answer:*
CLUELESS	CENTS	FUNNY BONE	SWELL

42. REPLACE TWO

The correct words are listed after the incorrect words.

1. shirk—shift
2. soft—raft
3. smart—small
4. place—grace
5. read—herd
6. ring—rank
7. born—work
8. brat—grab
9. flunk—skunk
10. helps—heads
11. charms—chores
12. dream—great
13. bulk—lull
14. angel—anvil
15. nasty—testy

43. AND COMING IN SECOND PLACE IS THE LETTER . . .
Answers will vary. These are suggestions:

bazaar	ajar	ostentatious
abrupt	ukulele	stride
accent	elegant	aura
adroit	emerging	every
lessen	annoyance	away
affluent	ooze	axle
aghast	epoxy	tyro
ahoy	aquamarine	ozone
ailment	arrest	

44. AN ICY SITUATION

1. ENTICE	6. POLICE	11. NICE
2. RICE	7. THRICE	12. SPICE
3. DICE	8. OFFICE	13. MICE
4. ADVICE	9. SUFFICE	14. VICE
5. PRICE	10. LICE	15. HOSPICE

45. DAYS AND MONTHS

1. MOON	6. NOVEL	11. FRISKY	16. MAROON
2. STUN	7. MARBLE	12. SLATE	17. DECIDE
3. WEED	8. DOCTOR	13. WEIRD	18. WIELD
4. JEANS	9. STUDENTS	14. AUGUR	19. SHATTER
5. OCTOPUS	10. FEEBLE	15. FRIED	20. APPROXIMATE

46. ANAGRAM ALLEY

1. icon	6. covert	11. diapers, despair	16. trainer
2. knee	7. vetoed	12. rentals	17. teaching
3. sham	8. cares, acres, races	13. ripples	18. serpent
4. brush	9. wolves	14. notices	19. omits
5. burden	10. kitchen	15. treason	20. canoe

47. MAKING A COMPOUND ELEMENTARY

1. THE: bartender	10. UAL: grandmother	19. EAN: shin splints
2. BES: basketball	11. WAY: homework	20. DTI: shopping
3. THI: beginning	12. SHU: hottest	21. DEW: stairway
4. NGS: broadcast	13. RTT: important	22. AIT: thinking
5. INL: championship	14. HEO: masthead	23. FOR: tornado
6. IFE: copyright	15. NEY: meantime	24. NOM: whatever
7. ARE: downstage	16. OUL: mockingbird	25. AN!: yourself
8. FRE: firsthand	17. OVE: newspaper	
9. EYO: forward	18. TIM: program	

The three sayings are: THE BEST THINGS IN LIFE ARE FREE. YOU ALWAYS HURT THE ONE YOU LOVE. TIME AND TIDE WAIT FOR NO MAN!

48. THE MISSING LETTER

1. capacity
2. artificial
3. foreign
4. guarantee
5. February
6. intelligent
7. fictitious
8. sophomore
9. antenna
10. curriculum
11. temperament
12. ecstacy
13. account
14. amount
15. apologize
16. winning
17. awkward
18. brought
19. allegiance
20. giraffe

The four animals are: TIGER, LION, RACCOON, WOLF

49. THE MISSING THREESOMES

1. courage
2. esteemed
3. fatigue
4. governor
5. happiness
6. inducement
7. justifiable
8. lovable
9. negotiate
10. occupant
11. ordinary
12. reference
13. remembrance
14. rhythm
15. substance
16. suspend
17. sustenance
18. tendency
19. university
20. unnecessary

50. IS IT DEADER THAN A HANGNAIL?

1. It was deader than a doornail.
2. He was a king skilled at playing the lyre.
3. The government of England was a limited monarchy.
4. Having two wives is called bigamy. Having one wife is called monogamy.
5. Those packages were sent by parcel post.
6. The inhabitants of Moscow are called Muscovites.
7. Indian squaws carried papooses on their backs.
8. It is customary to kiss the bride.
9. Let sleeping dogs lie.
10. The parents of Monica Green request your presence at the wedding.
11. Necessity is the mother of invention.
12. Never look a gift horse in the mouth.
13. Now the shoe is on the other foot.
14. All that glitters is not gold.
15. The movie is full of interesting characters.
16. A rolling stone gathers no moss.
17. Socrates died from an overdose of hemlock.
18. There is no time like the present.
19. You can lead a horse to water, but you can't make him drink.
20. That is a horse of a different color.

51. DID YOU WEAR YOUR CASHMERE SWEATER IN APRIL WHILE YOU DRANK CAPPUCCINO?

Numbers 1, 4, 10, 12, and 15 are true. Sources will vary.

52. GOING IN CIRCLES

There may be other words in addition to these:

ail	hickory	rider
ailing	ingot	rust
amazing	lam	rusty
ate	llama	rye
derail	low	stop
ell	lower	sty
era	pride	tell
gate	rail	tryst
got	railing	yell
gothic	rid	yellow
hick	ride	zing

53. START WITH IT, END WITH IT, AND ADD 3 IN BETWEEN

Answers may vary. These are suggestions:

blurb	fluff	level	rotor
cynic	going	madam	sexes
dread	hatch	ninon	tenet
eerie	kayak	primp	widow

54. FIND THE WORDS

Here are some words that can be formed. There may be others.

earn	near	swat	town	were
earth	newer	swear	warm	wizen
mare	rams	sweat	warn	wrath
math	size	Swiss	wart	wreath
more	swam	thaw	wear	wren
moth	swarm	torn	went	zero

55. YOUR QU IQ

A=4	B=15	C=10	D=5
E=6	F=9	G=16	H=3
I=13	J=2	K=7	L=12
M=11	N=8	O=1	P=14

The rows, columns, and diagonals add up to 34.

56. SS

Across:
- 4 PASS
- 6 DRESS
- 7 PROFESSOR
- 8 SUPPRESS
- 11 MESS
- 12 LISTLESS
- 14 SESSION
- 19 ASSIGN
- 21 PASSAGE
- 23 FLOSS
- 24 MESSY
- 25 DAUNTLESS

Down:
- 1 OPPRESS
- 2 COMPASS
- 3 LOSS
- 5 ASSESS
- 6 DEPRESS
- 9 STRESS
- 10 DISSOLVE
- 13 ASSESS
- 15 ASS
- 16 FUSSY
- 17 MASS
- 18 LASSY
- 20 GRASS
- 22 GLOSS

57. JUST DO IT!

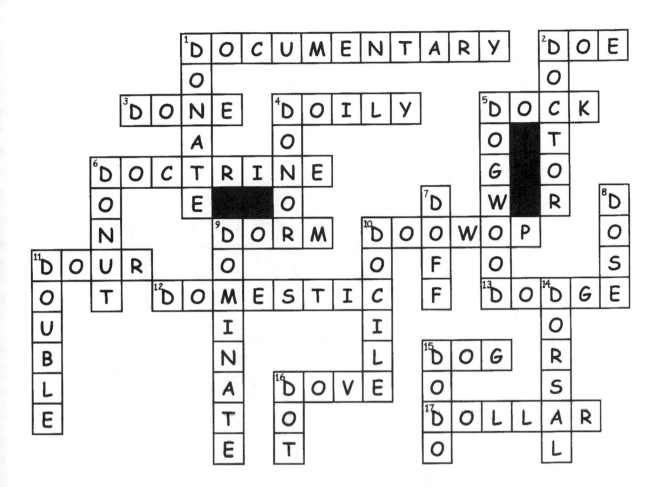

58. A+ ON THESE ANALOGIES

A=4	B=15	C=10	D=5
E=6	F=9	G=16	H=3
I=13	J=2	K=7	L=12
M=11	N=8	O=1	P=14

The rows, columns, and diagonals add up to 34.

Section Three: Getting Set for the Standards

59. THE BIG AND SMALL OF IT ALL

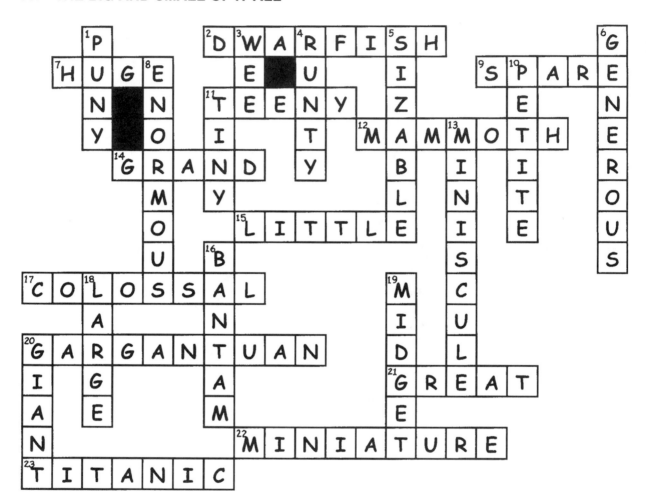

60. FIT TO A "T"

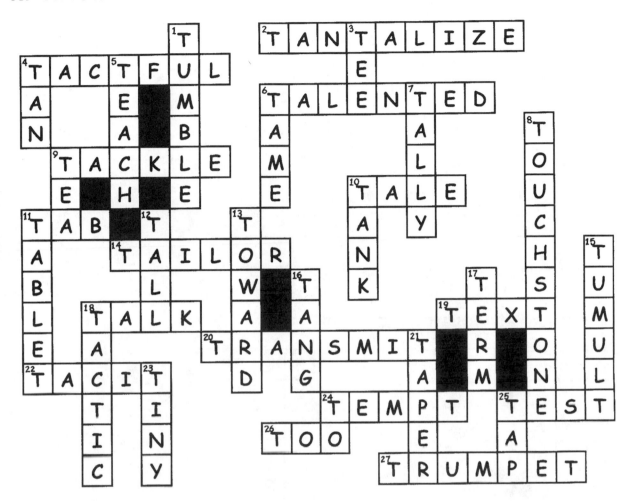

61. TWO CHARACTERS IN CONFLICT
Answers will vary.

62. ONE VERSUS THE CROWD
Answers will vary.

63. WORKING WITH QUOTES
Answers will vary.

64. MATCH THE MATE

A=4	B=10	C=17	D=14	E=20
F=15	G=18	H=23	I=2	J=7
K=21	L=1	M=13	N=25	O=5
P=19	Q=24	R=3	S=8	T=11
U=6	V=12	W=9	X=16	Y=22

The columns, rows, and diagonals add up to 65.

65. ROOTING FOR YOU WITH THE ROOTS

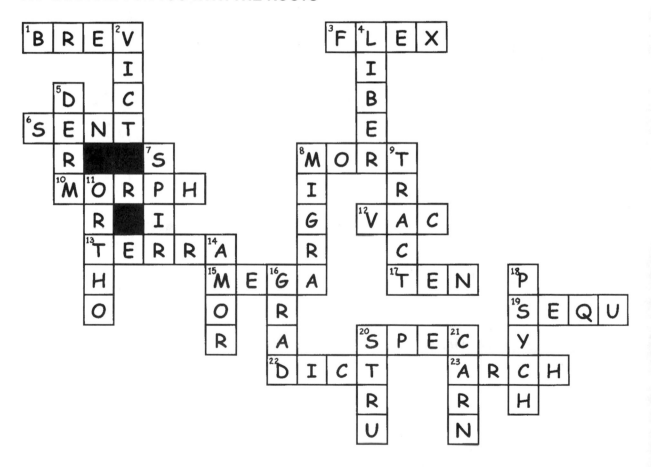

The students' words for each root will vary.

66. MISSING-LETTER MAGIC SQUARE

A=4	B=10	C=17	D=14	E=20
F=15	G=18	H=23	I=2	J=7
K=21	L=1	M=13	N=25	O=5
P=19	Q=24	R=3	S=8	T=11
U=6	V=12	W=9	X=16	Y=22

The columns, rows, and diagonals add up to 65.

67. PI

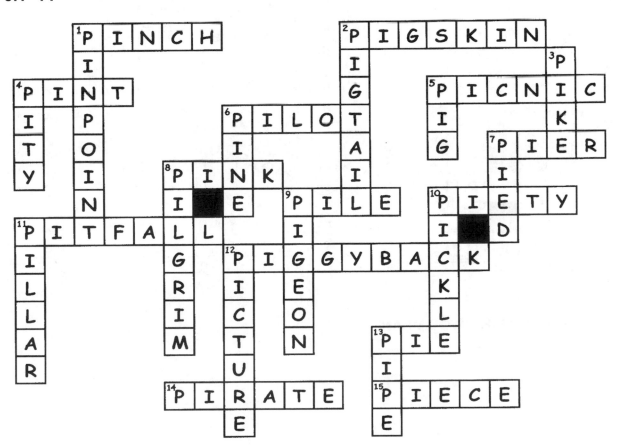

68. I SPENT THE NIGHT IN THE . . .

1. BUNGALOW
2. HOTEL
3. COTTAGE
4. VILLA
5. MANSION
6. TENT
7. MOTEL
8. CABIN
9. HUT
10. CHALET
11. HOSPICE
12. PALACE
13. TRAILER
14. CASTLE
15. LONGHOUSE
16. TENEMENT
17. INN
18. IGLOO
19. HOUSEBOAT
20. TOWNHOUSE
21. FLAT
22. APARTMENT
23. CONDOMINIUM
24. TREEHUT
25. TEPEE

Sub:	A	B	C	D	E	F	G	H	I	L	M	N	O	P	R	S	T	U	V	W
Real:	S	E	V	T	F	P	N	M	I	A	O	B	D	U	C	R	W	L	G	H

69. JAM-PACKED

70. SHOWING WHAT YOU MEAN

Answers will vary.

71.   KNOWING ADE IS YOUR AID

A=13	B=3	C=6	D=12
E=8	F=10	G=15	H=1
I=11	J=5	K=4	L=14
M=2	N=16	O=9	P=7

The rows, columns, and diagonals add up to 34.

72.   HEAR OUR THE ERAS
1. He threw the ball through the window.
2. We plan to meet you later, Lesley.
3. The bee smelled the scent of the beautiful garden flower.
4. When I pushed my foot down on the car's brake, I hurt my heel.
5. Has she heard what the poor people need for the holidays?
6. Bill scraped his knee on the coarse board too.
7. Who is the one who painted this pretty scene?
8. The company's quiet personnel director seldom wastes words.
9. Would you change your plans if the weather turns nasty?
10. Ken has a right to write what he thinks about war and peace.
11. There will be a minor change in the way they manufacture steel.
12. When you find it, use the organization's official stationery.
13. The moral of the story involves real pain and sacrifice.
14. Her aunt's favorite color is blue, and her favorite dessert is vanilla ice cream.
15. Did his compliment about your recent weight loss affect you?

73.   FIRST AND THIRD
1. ADAMANT
2. BOBBY
3. CACTUS
4. DADDY
5. ELEGANT
6. FIFTY
7. GIGANTIC
8. HAH
9. INITIAL
10. LOLLYPOP (or LOLLIPOP)
11. MEMBER
12. NONCONFORMIST
13. OZONE
14. PAPER
15. RARITY
16. SYSTEM
17. TITLE
18. UKULELE
19. VIVID
20. YOYO

74. A TO Z ON BOTH SIDES

acme / pinnacle
bastion / citadel
circular / round
dagger / knife
element / xenon
falsehood / lie
gifted / talented
hazy / misty
incarcerate / imprison

jolt / shake
kudos /endorsement
lapse /decline
mark / gash
noise / babble
onset / first
pagan / heathen
quiver / jerk
rapidity / quickness

slay / zap
tell / narrate
ultimatum / order
voluminous / unabridged
woeful / wretched
xanthous / yellowish
yacht /vessel
zone / area

75. DOUBLE-LETTER DILEMMAS

1. session
2. babble
3. vacuum
4. muffle
5. happy
6. bazaar
7. dazzle
8. mutter
9. savvy
10. bookkeeper
11. hammer
12. noodle
13. gaggle
14. hurry
15. moccasin
16. fiddle
17. hello
18. radii
19. cheer
20. annoy

76. HOW PROUD!

1. opal
2. char
3. opus
4. ecru
5. rude
6. peso
7. tort
8. soil
9. onus
10. diva
11. pile
12. tire
13. alto
14. must
15. eddy
16. pale
17. odor
18. tyro
19. bunk
20. arid

77. BOXING THEM IN

HONESTY: fairness, integrity, objectiveness, probity, rectitude, uprightness
OBEDIENCE: abidance, acquiescence, allegiance, compliance, conformity, yielding
PARDON: allowance, clemency, compassion, indulgence, lenience, mercifulness
RANDOM: arbitrary, casual, desultory, haphazard, irregular, willy-nilly
SMALL: bantam, diminutive, insignificant, miniscule, slender, tiny

78. OUR SPELL-CHECK IS BROKEN

```
y  m  x  f  c  k  p  y  l  u  f  i  t  n  u  o  b  l  f
s  u  o  d  n  e  r  r  o  h  h  r  p  s  s  d  v  u  w
c  s  y  m  p  a  t  h  e  t  i  c  u  c  q  n  j  f  l
j  z  l  b  d  h  m  m  c  l  x  y  s  i  n  n  s  i  w
d  p  g  n  s  k  f  h  b  n  h  r  r  g  t  m  q  t  s
y  s  u  s  b  y  w  z  n  h  h  z  l  y  e  f  c  n  s
h  o  z  s  l  p  m  d  f  t  h  y  s  l  k  o  u  e  s
b  v  f  e  i  h  c  s  i  m  g  r  a  m  m  a  r  l  p
n  d  v  r  v  g  x  t  p  o  w  n  d  m  x  t  i  p  a
q  o  i  t  p  u  m  f  l  e  c  j  i  t  h  g  g  n  t
l  y  c  s  y  o  p  a  g  h  c  s  d  g  h  z  p  k  h
q  w  i  m  k  r  n  t  o  r  s  i  u  t  j  m  c  m  e
f  b  o  a  p  a  b  l  k  i  z  o  a  w  s  b  g  x  t
d  v  u  e  z  z  y  m  o  w  r  c  j  l  g  l  f  j  i
k  n  s  s  v  w  c  n  z  w  l  u  s  c  i  o  u  s  c
```

analogy	fruitful	luscious	plentiful	sympathetic
boundary	grammar	melancholy	wrought	slight
bountiful	horrendous	mischief	rough	special
commission	lovely	pathetic	seamstress	vicious

79. GETTING INTO TOPIC SENTENCES

The following are the topic sentences with the opinion listed after the topic:

2. Smoking . . . harmful to your health
3. *Johnny Tremain* . . . . interesting book for seventh graders
4. Michael Jordan . . . undoubtedly the world's greatest athlete
5. Mathematics . . . can be a difficult subject
10. "Francine's" . . . tastiest meals in town
11. You . . . one of the friendliest people I have ever met
12. This car . . . too expensive

The students' sentences will vary.

80. HE AND I OR HIM AND ME?

1. her (IC)
2. he (ES)
3. she (LE)
4. them (DS)
5. who (NO)
6. you (WB)
7. yourself (OA)
8. Everybody (RD)
9. Much (IN)
10. they (GS)
11. whomever (KI)
12. She (IN)
13. yourself (GS)
14. All (KA)
15. he (TE)

The five words associated with cold weather: ICE, SLED, SNOWBOARDING, SKIING, SKATE.

81. MAKING SENSE OF THESE SENTENCES

1. (B) versatility
2. (C) unexpected
3. (B) little
4. (D) compromise
5. (C) diligent
6. (A) unified
7. (C) verbose
8. (B) turbulent
9. (A) ridicule
10. (C) champion
11. spiteful
12. unpalatable
13. rashly
14. precipitous
15. connoisseur

82. SEEING RED

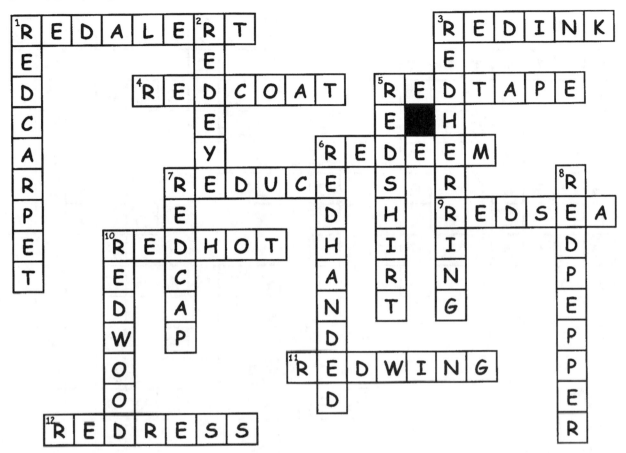

83. WE HAD DESSERT ON THE PLANE

1. a(l)lowance
2. d(i)scipline
3. a(s)cent
4. a(b)breviate
5. p(o)isonous
6. i(n)telligent
7. n(o)ticeable

8. e(s)capade
9. p(l)easant
10. s(o)los
11. r(a)bid
12. e(n)couraging
13. u(k)ulele
14. p(a)ralyzed

15. p(r)ecious
16. l(a)boratory
17. f(l)exible
18. d(i)sturbing
19. o(m)itted
20. c(a)lendar

The four world capitals: LISBON (Portugal), OSLO (Norway), ANKARA (Turkey), LIMA (Peru)

84. GAS AND OIL

A crossword puzzle grid with the following answers:

Across:
- OSCILLATE
- ORIGINAL
- FOIBLE
- ROIL
- EMBROIL
- SOIL
- DOILY
- GASKET
- AGHAST
- GLASS
- GEARS
- GRATES

Down:
- BOIL
- GALL
- OIL
- TURMOIL
- COOL
- FOIL
- BROIL
- RIOTS
- SPOIL
- BROIL
- OPTIONAL
- GLASS
- GRASP
- GLARES

Section Four: Really Writing and Really Discussing

85. IDIOMS (PART ONE)

These are the "accepted" meanings of the idioms. The student's creativity and thinking skills in making up derivations are more important than knowing the actual derivation.

1. Make peace
2. Make a start; get better acquainted
3. All inclusive
4. Doing something difficult
5. Pay attention to details
6. It didn't work out
7. Any way possible
8. Things were halted in the nick of time
9. Make a fresh start
10. Pursuing something not relevant

86. IDIOMS (PART TWO)

These are the "accepted" meanings of the idioms. The student's creativity and thinking skills in making up derivations are more important than knowing the actual derivation.

1. support an already popular cause or idea
2. to be "admitted" another day
3. have a negative attitude
4. happens infrequently
5. done very quickly and quietly
6. to be treated in a special way
7. get down to business
8. a gift or possession that's unwanted or out of place
9. be in sync with others
10. limiting your possibilities by focusing in only one area

87. EXAMINING EMILY

Answers will vary.

88. WHAT IS A GOOD BOOK?

Answers will vary.

89. WHERE DID IT COME FROM?

Answers will vary.

90. TELL THE STORY BEHIND IT

1. **bite the bullet** (to confront a difficult situation bravely): In order to relieve pain and take the Civil War injured soldier's mind off the possible incision or amputation that the soldier was to undergo because of a serious wound, the soldier was told to bite on a bullet.

2. **back to square one** (to do away with what you have already done and to start over): In board games, all players had to start at the same place on the board, the first square or square one. If the player rolled the dice and was told to go back to the beginning of the board, he/she went back to square one. The idea of starting the game over also meant going back to square one.

3. **double-cross** (to betray): In America's early days, a person unable to write his own name was allowed to sign a legal document with an "X." When this illiterate person did not fully agree to the terms of the document or when he was forced to sign this document, he would write an additional X or double-cross (two X's).

4. **bring home the bacon** (to earn a living; to succeed or win): Rural Americans enjoyed their country fairs. One popular activity was the greased pig contest, an event in which the person who caught the slippery greased pig could take it home as a prize for his efforts. Since a pig is the source of bacon, the winner of the greased pig contest could "bring home the bacon."

91. THREE CHARACTERS
Answers will vary.

92. DRAW THE DESCRIPTIONS
Drawings will vary, but should resemble the descriptions given.

93. FOR OPENERS (PART ONE)
Answers will vary.

94. FOR OPENERS (PART TWO)
Answers will vary.

95. PARAPHRASING POWER
Answers will vary.

96. "FUNERAL BLUES"

1. Metaphors include: He was my North, my South, my East and West, My working week and my Sunday rest; My noon, my midnight, my talk, my song

2. The poet is comparing seemingly unlike things.

3. First-person point of view

4. clocks—cut (line 1); barking—bone (line 2); coffin—come (line 3); Scribbling—sky (line 6); my North, my South, my East (line 9); My working week and my Sunday rest (line 10); My noon, my midnight, my talk, my song (line 11); love—last (line 12);

was wrong (line 12); not wanted now (line 13); nothing now (line 16); can—come (line 16)

5. The answers to question 4 would also apply here.
6. The tone of the poem is sad.
7. The many images of death and stoppage of activity point to sadness.
8. The first three lines of the third stanza include examples of repetition.
9. Repetition is used often for emphasis. In this case, the poet emphasizes the deep hurt that this death has brought him.
10. The setting appears to be at a wake or a funeral. If not that specific, it is on some obviously sad occasion.
11. The rhyme scheme is *aabb ccdd eeff gghh*.
12. A symbol is the clock. On a literal level, a clock tells time. On the figurative level, the clock's stopping means that time is no longer functioning or important after the person's death. Other symbols that could be discussed certainly include the telephone (line 2), crepe bows (line 7), white necks (line 7), public doves (line 7), black cotton gloves (line 8), all the directions on line 9, the many images in the third stanza, and the celestial bodies in the concluding stanza.
13. The images are mostly depressing since they point to closure or stoppage of life's activity. Warmth, light, and communication will disappear.
14. There are many examples of sound devices. The monosyllabic words such as "Stop" (line 1) and "cut off" (line 1) point to the immediacy and finalization of the death. Other words, including "Silence" (line 3), have a soothing sound. The "moaning" (line 5) sound matches the sense of death well. "Put out" (line 13), "Pour away" (line 15), and "sweep up" (line 15) also connote the intended sense of finality effectively.

97. THE DESERT ISLAND

Answers will vary.

98. TOWNS

Answers will vary. These are possible suggestions:

1. (A) There had been racial riots in 1965. Today, there are many vacant stores in the town. Unemployment is apparent. (B) Unemployment is evident due to the factories closing down. There is restlessness today. The mines that had been so fruitful are now barren.
2. Racial riots.
3. The mines have been stripped and are now barren.
4. The narrator had sat on his father's lap as a child, and now the narrator's son is doing the same with the narrator.
5. The promises that had been made to the youth of Allentown were never carried out. Today their graduation diplomas hang on the wall, virtually useless. The mines are empty, and the unemployment lines are long and full. This generation will probably never be as successful as the previous generation because they lack jobs and means of making a productive living in Allentown. It appears that people will be leaving Allentown, if they have not already done so.
6. Both talk about disappointment. Both address the conflicts inherent in the towns. Both talk about leaving the town.
7. Springsteen's town's past was full of racial strife. Allentown's past held much promise for the future.

8. Racial riots, a shooting, and a drive through the town are prevalent images.
9. World War II images, productive mines, closed factories, and unemployment lines are prevalent images.

99. SENSING WHAT IS GOING ON
Answers will vary.

100. YOU DO HAVE A CLUE!
Answers will vary.

101. THE AUTHOR'S MESSAGE
Answers will vary.

102. A PURPOSE TO EVERY WORD AND EVERY SENTENCE
Answers will vary.

103. WHAT HAVE WE LEARNED?
Answers will vary.

104. WR SE QU DI
Answers will vary. These are suggestions:

1. They have always had many exciting times with their friends.
2. When will you finish the project?
3. Her mother can drive the bus tomorrow.
4. Save the last dance for him.
5. Have you seen that movie yet?
6. Bring her pocketbook back with you.
7. She always attends sporting events and musical concerts.
8. There were only twelve children there.
9. Foreign exchange students will select their classes next week.
10. Why have these animals not eaten yet?

105. TACKLING THESE TOUGH TOPICS
Answers will vary.

106. HOW WILL IT TURN OUT?
Answers will vary.

107. PASSING IT ALONG
Answers will vary.

108. I'D PICK . . .
Answers will vary.

Section Five: Critical Thinking Is Critical!

109. COMPUTERESE

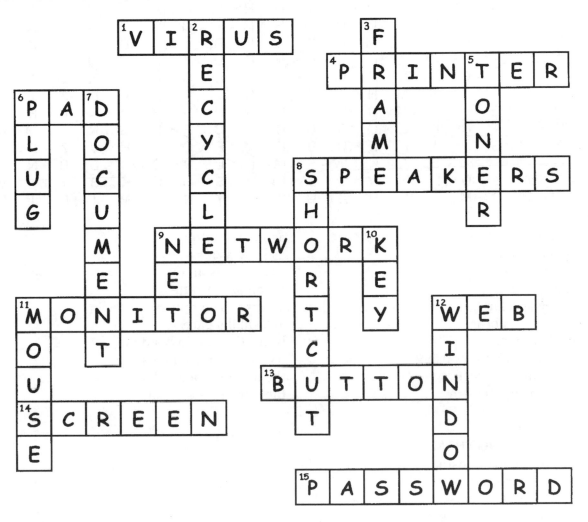

110. AS THE ANIMALS GO

```
B  J  L  Z  W  V  Q  B  S  L  Q  Z  B  Y  G  W  Y  B  D  Y
K  Q  N  N  Q  D  D  X  M  T  P  V  W  G  I  M  P  B  D  B
X  Y  V  Z  F  C  G  B  N  H  U  Q  S  H  R  D  B  R  Y  L
C  Q  H  S  J  R  J  N  D  Y  D  R  W  B  A  S  Q  P  T  R
D  H  N  Y  F  S  L  D  G  H  M  T  Q  F  F  H  N  V  X  K
J  U  U  L  C  T  K  M  I  W  E  D  B  L  F  D  N  A  Z  S
T  A  C  R  F  O  X  L  O  O  N  D  U  Y  E  G  O  T  I  W
P  J  V  K  C  O  N  X  L  P  N  J  L  Q  R  Q  N  G  T  L
C  V  P  R  D  H  M  H  A  X  E  S  L  B  J  A  D  X  Y  M
S  N  L  Q  V  N  M  D  M  S  D  A  N  B  H  R  N  L  B  S
D  W  L  A  R  K  J  O  B  C  B  Q  C  P  I  G  R  J  M  N
O  B  W  G  J  J  P  E  U  B  P  M  E  O  C  R  V  Z  F  M
H  G  W  F  X  D  A  K  W  S  M  L  L  N  C  S  D  B  N  Q
T  D  T  Z  D  R  Y  M  Z  Z  E  V  S  G  N  K  B  Y  Y  V
X  S  M  Q  M  T  Q  H  Z  D  D  P  Y  N  T  M  J  M  J  B
```

as a <u>duck</u> takes to water
as clever as a <u>fox</u>
as crazy as a <u>loon</u>
as free as a <u>bird</u>
as happy as a <u>lark</u>
as hungry as a <u>bear</u>
as meek as a <u>lamb</u>
as poor as a <u>churchmouse</u>
as proud as a <u>peacock</u>
as scarce as <u>hen</u>'s teeth

as sick as a <u>dog</u>
as slow as a <u>turtle</u>
as strong as an <u>ox</u>
as tall as a <u>giraffe</u>
as wise as an <u>owl</u>
at a <u>snail</u>'s pace
beard the <u>lion</u> in his den
like a <u>bull</u> in a china shop
the memory of an <u>elephant</u>
the nine lives of a <u>cat</u>

111. GROUPING THEM

1. football positions
2. musical terms
3. parts of speech
4. freshwater fish
5. most common words in spoken English
6. inventors
7. Elvis Presley hit songs
8. types of teeth
9. famous years in American history (1776: birthday of the U.S.; 1865: end of the Civil War; 1929: Stock Market crash; 1945: end of WWII)
10. punctuation marks
11. types of dogs
12. hairstyles
13. computer terms
14. past participles of irregular verbs
15. capital cities of American states

112. FIGHTING A LIAR: SPOONERISMS

1. Lighting a fire
2. Steady as a rock
3. You missed my history lecture
4. Battle ships and cruisers
5. Cozy little nook
6. Our dear old queen
7. We'll have the flags hung out
8. You wasted two terms
9. Our loving shepherd
10. Is the dean busy?
11. Go and take a shower
12. Ease my tears
13. You have very bad manners
14. Pack of lies
15. Healing the sick
16. So help me God
17. I'm a stamp dealer
18. Save the whales
19. I was flipping the channels on the TV
20. Bad money

113. BROADWAY BOUND

A=2	B=3	C=15	D=14
E=13	F=16	G=4	H=1
I=8	J=5	K=9	L=12
M=11	N=10	O=6	P=7

The columns, rows, and diagonals add up to 34.

114. IN OTHER WORDS

Answers will vary.

115. SEEING DOUBLE

1. Bob/bob
2. Carol/carol
3. Don/don
4. Art/art
5. Eddy/eddy
6. Frank/frank
7. Guy/guy
8. Iris/iris
9. Sue/sue
10. Win/win
11. Ray/ray
12. Victor/victor
13. Hector/hector
14. Laurel/laurel
15. Curt/curt
16. Rich/rich
17. Mark/mark
18. Drew/drew
19. Jack/jack
20. Venus/Venus

116. LITERARY CHARACTERS IN OTHER SETTINGS

Answers will vary.

117. SOUNDS LIKE A PROVERB BUT . . .

2. Old habits die hard.
3. Robbing Peter to pay Paul.
4. No news is good news.
5. Never look a gift horse in the mouth.
6. Better be safe than sorry.
7. Many hands make light work.
8. Let sleeping dogs lie.
9. Great minds think alike.
10. All's fair in love and war.
11. A man's home is his castle.
12. Slow and steady wins the race.
13. Seeing is believing.
14. Walls have ears.
15. Time cures all things.
16. Still water runs deep.
17. Spare the rod and spoil the child.
18. Turn the other cheek.
19. Bad news travels fast.
20. Fight fire with fire.

118. A MIXED-UP WORLD

Answers will vary.

119. LUCKY 13

Answers will vary.

120. FIND THE FOUR AND SCORE

1. quiz
2. kick
3. itch
4. jump
5. open
6. bake
7. ruin
8. xray
9. boat
10. yawn
11. find
12. loll
13. talk
14. zero
15. mind
16. grow
17. stay
18. ache
19. flay
20. nuke
21. urge
22. dust
23. rest
24. cook
25. hire

Code Helper																									
Sub:	R	K	I	J	O	B	S	X	W	Y	F	L	U	Z	M	G	T	A	P	N	V	D	Q	C	H	E
Real:	A	B	C	D	E	F	G	H	I	J	K	L	M	N	O	P	Q	R	S	T	U	V	W	X	Y	Z

121. CAUSE AND EFFECT

1. D
2. B
3. B
4. C
5. A case can be made for A and a case can be made for D. The length of time (10 days) might suggest no causal relationship.
6. probably A
7. D
8. C. Ninety-five percent of all cocaine addicts also drank milk as children. The milk didn't cause the cocaine use.
9. C. You can make a case for A if it can be established that the climate impacts positively on longevity.
10. A

122. **NOT JUST THE FACTS**
1. Opinion
2. Generalization (contains the word "most")
3. Fact
4. Opinion. The word "important" makes this statement an opinion, although it's an opinion a large percentage of the population would probably embrace.
5. There are two statements here. Both are opinions; however, an argument could be made that the second statement is an inference drawn from the first.
6. Inference. The second statement is a judgment based on the observation spoken about the first statement.
7. Opinion (define "very reclusive")
8. Fact
9. You can make a case for inference, based on observation; fact, they told you so; opinion, you think so because of how many years they've been together.
10. Opinion (define "cold")

123. **JUST BECAUSE**
1. Just because Dr. Jones has celebrity endorsements doesn't mean he is a good surgeon. The celebrities could be paid for their endorsements.
2. It is very difficult to prove a negative. There may be life on other planets. Just because no one has disproved it, however, does not make it so.
3. Just because there is not enough evidence to convict Mr. Smith doesn't mean he is innocent.
4. Just because more people own something doesn't make it the best. Maybe it is very inexpensive.
5. Just because doing something makes us feel nostalgic does not mean it is the right thing to do.
6. Friends losing their jobs are something to be concerned about, but just because they will keep their jobs if Senator Lawlor gets elected does not make him the best candidate.
7. Just because they voted against it two years ago does not mean it is still a bad idea. Circumstances may have changed.
8. An idea should be judged on its own merit, not in terms of the person or group advocating it.
9. Just because nobody has said anything positive about someone doesn't mean that people have negative feelings. They simply may not have spoken about him at all.
10. Just because we have done something wrong doesn't mean we should ignore similar wrongdoing. Two wrongs do not make a right.

124. **LOGIC PROBLEMS**
1. Alan: quarterback; Bob: tight end: Casey: halfback
2. Christine and Ted; Alexis and Bill; Ellen and Joe
3. Aaron: floor exercise; Barry: parallel bars; Chuck: rings; Dave: horse
4. Bob and Mary; Jim and Kristen; Frank and Amy

125. **IT'S ALL IN THE NAME**
Answers will vary.

126. R U O-K?

1. The exam is easy.
2. This is the cure.
3. You are the one, Jay.
4. Anyone see Artie?
5. I am too busy for you.
6. Why are you dizzy?
7. You are a cutie, Alex!
8. He is examining the eyes.
9. The bee is the enemy.
10. It's empty, Dee!
11. Is this ecstasy?
12. The tea is for you.
13. See the beady eyes?
14. I can double you, Henry.
15. The biscuits are for you.

127. HELP!

1. abet
2. boost
3. free
4. back
5. ease
6. aid
7. sustain
8. oblige
9. succor
10. favor
11. enhance
12. assist
13. rescue
14. support
15. contribute
16. subsidize
17. endorse
18. sanction
19. accommodate
20. collaborate

Letter Substitution Code

Code:	A	B	C	D	E	F	G	H	I	K	L	M	N	O	P	R	S	T	U	V	Z
Real:	R	V	P	H	B	F	U	Z	E	D	S	K	L	C	I	O	A	M	T	N	G

---

128. WONDERING WHAT IT MEANS

Answers will vary.

129. ALLITERATIVE SLOGANS

Answers will vary.

130. RHYMING YOUR TIME AWAY

1. wives' knives
2. brave slave
3. funny money
4. loud crowd
5. sick wick
6. square pair
7. round ground
8. Herbert's sherbets
9. Molly's trolleys
10. Pole's roles
11. Starr's jars
12. Andes' candies
13. Bill's tills
14. snake's fakes
15. glad dad
16. Thomas's promises
17. boar's roars
18. first thirst
19. great mate
20. Mike's likes

131. ALL IN A LINE NOW!

1. (QU) airport
2. (EU) backstab
3. (EI) blacksmith
4. (SA) candlestick
5. (WO) downtown
6. (RD) dustpan
7. (WH) elbowroom
8. (OS) football
9. (EL) friendship
10. (AS) grandstand
11. (TF) headline
12. (OU) highway
13. (RL) masthead
14. (ET) padlock
15. (TE) pocketbook
16. (RS) riverbank
17. (AR) straightedge
18. (ES) sweatshirt
19. (IL) tenderfoot
20. (EN) weatherproof
21. (T!) workbench

The sentence reads: QUEUE IS A WORD WHOSE LAST FOUR LETTERS ARE SILENT! (Since a *queue* is a line, the activity's title "All in a Line Now!" makes sense.)

132. THINKING CRITICALLY WITH WORDS
These are suggested answers:
1. The word "stone" can be added to each word.
2. Each word is a palindrome.
3. The prefix "bi-" can be added to each word.
4. The letter "l" can replace the first "r" in each word.
5. Each word has the same consonant in slots 1, 3, and 4.
6. Each word starts with consecutive letters of the alphabet.
7. Each word's first and last letters are consecutive letters of the alphabet.

133. MORE THINKING CRITICALLY WITH WORDS
These are suggested answers:
1. Each word's last letter is silent.
2. The suffix "-less" can be added to each word.
3. There is a double letter in each word.
4. The prefix "sea-" can be added to each word.
5. The prefix "be-" can be added to each word.
6. The word "French" can be placed before each word.

Section Six: Researching and Remembering

134. AND WHERE DID THIS ONE COME FROM? (PART ONE)

A=2	B=3	C=15	D=14
E=13	F=16	G=4	H=1
I=8	J=5	K=9	L=12
M=11	N=10	O=6	P=7

The rows, columns, and diagonals add up to 34.

135. AND WHERE DID THIS ONE COME FROM? (PART TWO)

A=11	B=13	C=8	D=2
E=4	F=6	G=15	H=9
I=5	J=3	K=10	L=16
M=14	N=12	O=1	P=7

The rows, columns, and diagonals add up to 34.

136. AND WHERE DID THIS ONE COME FROM? (PART THREE)

A=11	B=13	C=8	D=2
E=4	F=6	G=15	H=9
I=5	J=3	K=10	L=16
M=14	N=12	O=1	P=7

The rows, columns, and diagonals add up to 34.

137. FAMOUS YOUNG PEOPLE

A=1	B=15	C=8	D=10
E=4	F=14	G=5	H=11
I=13	J=3	K=12	L=6
M=16	N=2	O=9	P=7

The rows, columns, and diagonals add up to 34.

138. AWARD-WINNING MUSICIANS

A=6	B=2	C=13	D=24	E=20
F=14	G=25	H=16	I=7	J=3
K=17	L=8	M=4	N=15	O=21
P=5	Q=11	R=22	S=18	T=9
U=23	V=19	W=10	X=1	Y=12

The rows, columns, and diagonals add up to 65.

139. LOOK IT UP (ROUND ONE)
1. Poland
2. Amherst
3. Hercule Poirot
4. A. A. Milne
5. Guinevere
6. Louis XIV
7. *The Mystery of Edwin Drood*
8. Mr. Rochester
9. Doris Lessing
10. Venice
11. James Whistler
12. Charles Lindbergh
13. Geriatrics
14. queue
15. Vishnu, the preserver god
16. Faust
17. Charles M. Schulz
18. twelve
19. Texas
20. on the moon

140. LOOK IT UP (ROUND TWO)

1. Korean War
2. Portugal
3. Florence Nightingale
4. eight
5. birds
6. every year
7. the Philippines
8. India
9. Tennyson
10. badminton
11. Billy Joel
12. fourteen
13. NBC (National Broadcasting Company)
14. Oklahoma
15. e
16. basketball
17. Monopoly
18. 26
19. Wings
20. Elmira, New York

141. CHALLENGING QUOTATIONS

1. Isaac Newton
2. *To Kill a Mockingbird*
3. Herbert Hoover
4. George Santayana
5. (C) Veni, Vidi, Vici.
6. Mark Twain
7. Anne Boleyn
8. *Rebecca*
9. John F. Kennedy
10. Abraham Lincoln

142. CAN YOU FIND IT?

1. Larry Walker of the Colorado Rockies
2. New York
3. the lira
4. Anne Hathaway
5. Dwight David Eisenhower
6. mouth (a bicuspid is a tooth)
7. Steven Spielberg
8. money
9. Dr. Seuss
10. Denmark
11. six
12. slow
13. tennis
14. the 19th
15. 220 yards, or 201.2 meters, or 1/8 of a mile

143. THE RESEARCH PROVES IT

A=1	B=10	C=19	D=23	E=12
F=18	G=22	H=11	I=5	J=9
K=15	L=4	M=8	N=17	O=21
P=7	Q=16	R=25	S=14	T=3
U=24	V=13	W=2	X=6	Y=20

The columns, rows, and diagonals add up to 65.

144. **TOPICS**
Answers will vary.

145. **FAMOUS PEOPLE**

A=13	B=3	C=6	D=12
E=8	F=10	G=15	H=1
I=11	J=5	K=4	L=14
M=2	N=16	O=9	P=7

The columns, rows, and diagonals add up to 34.

146. **LOUIE IS LOST!**

A=15	B=6	C=9	D=4
E=12	F=1	G=14	H=7
I=2	J=11	K=8	L=13
M=5	N=16	O=3	P=10

The columns, rows, and diagonals add up to 34.

147. **THE TYPES OF READING MATERIALS**

1. H	6. J	11. E
2. A	7. B	12. L
3. I	8. O	13. N
4. C	9. K	14. D
5. G	10. F	15. M

148. YOU AND YOUR SURROUNDINGS

Answers will vary.

149. ADD THEM UP!

1. 3 + 4 + 14 = 21
2. 1 + 2 + 5 = 8
3. 8 + 9 + 10 = 27
4. 4 + 7 + 20 + 1 = 32
5. 100 + 5 + 9 = 114
6. 10 + 6 + 1000 = 1016
7. 5 + 10 + 80 = 95
8. 3 + 4 + 10 = 17
9. 4 + 5 + 100 = 109
10. 1 + 20 + 10 = 31
11. 10 + 1600 = 1610
12. 100 + 10 = 110
13. 50 + 6 = 56
14. 1776 + 8 + 10 = 1794
15. 10 + 9 + 4 = 23

150. DO YOU KNOW THE U.S.?

1. T
2. H
3. E
4. S
5. E
6. A
7. R
8. S
9. T
10. O
11. W
12. E
13. R
14. C
15. H
16. I
17. C
18. A
19. G
20. O

The famous U.S. landmark: THE SEARS TOWER, CHICAGO

151. REALLY RESEARCHING

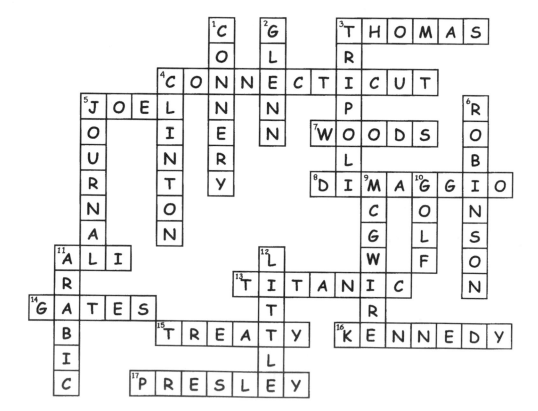

152. WHAT A YEAR!

1. N	5. J	9. D	13. F
2. H	6. I	10. L	14. A
3. E	7. P	11. G	15. O
4. B	8. M	12. K	16. C

153. THE MISSING LINK

A=4	B=10	C=17	D=14	E=20
F=15	G=18	H=23	I=2	J=7
K=21	L=1	M=13	N=25	O=5
P=19	Q=24	R=3	S=8	T=11
U=6	V=12	W=9	X=16	Y=22

The columns, rows, and diagonals add up to 65.

154. NUMBERS

A=12	B=13	C=1	D=8
E=6	F=3	G=15	H=10
I=7	J=2	K=14	L=11
M=9	N=16	O=4	P=5

The columns, rows, and diagonals add up to 34.

155. LITERARY HUNT

1. "Tiger, Tiger"	5. Marjorie Kinnan Rawlings	9. New York
2. Emily Dickinson	6. J. K. Rowling	10. H. H. Munro
3. David Copperfield	7. 14	11. Noel Coward
4. Doctor Watson	8. 17	12. e e cummings

156. BY THE NUMBERS

A=11	B=22	C=18	D=9	E=5
F=8	G=4	H=15	I=21	J=17
K=25	L=16	M=7	N=3	O=14
P=2	Q=13	R=24	S=20	T=6
U=19	V=10	W=1	X=12	Y=23

The columns, rows, and diagonals add up to 65.

Section Seven: You Are Special

157. YOU AND A FRIEND
Answers will vary.

158. WHAT DO YOUR ANSWERS TELL YOU?
Answers will vary.

159. CONNECTING YOUR THOUGHTS
Answers will vary.

160. A WAY WITH WORDS
Stories will vary, but must include the 15 words in order.

161. GET YOUR HEAD INTO THIS ACTIVITY
1. arm
2. back
3. knuckle
4. shoulder
5. neck
6. hand
7. ear
8. knee
9. jaw
10. leg
11. lip
12. foot, mouth
13. face
14. elbow
15. stomach

162. DRAW AND ENJOY
Drawings will vary.

163. YOUR BEDROOM
Stories will vary.

164. GRANNY AND ODLUM'S
Stories will vary.

165. START THE WORLD'S NEXT CIVILIZATION
Answers will vary.

166. EXACTLY WHO ARE YOU?
Answers will vary.

167. HOW MUCH ARE YOU LIKE YOUR FRIENDS AND CLASSMATES?
Answers will vary.

168. IF I WERE . . .
Answers will vary.

169. THINKING LITERARILY
Answers will vary.

170. WHAT WILL THE FUTURE BRING?
Answers will vary.

171. HOW GOOD CAN ONE BE?
Answers will vary.

172. WHAT WOULD THEY DO?
Answers will vary.

173. TRY THESE TEN TOUGH TONGUE TWISTERS TODAY
Answers will vary.

174.   JUST DROPPING IN
Answers will vary.

175.   DISCUSSING AND DECIDING
Answers will vary.

176.   EACH THREE WILL HELP YOU TO SEE (MORE ABOUT YOURSELF)
Answers will vary.

177.   BUILD THE PERFECT PERSON
Answers will vary.

178.   THINKING AND WRITING
Answers will vary.

179.   THE DESCRIPTIVE YOU
Answers will vary.

180.   THE PERFECT DAY
Answers will vary.

181.   WOULD YOU RATHER . . . ?
Answers will vary.